ENDORSEMENTS

"I have known Dave Chapman for over 50 years and count him a good friend and solid co-laborer in the gospel of Jesus Christ. When I was Senior Pastor of Crossroads Bible Church in Bellevue, Washington he helped our church set up an outreach ministry that both trained and saved many people in our area. Our leadership team found Dave to be so faithful that we asked him to plant a church in a close city to ours and base the ministry on a strong evangelist foundation. Dave has a big heart for the lost of this world and his book on evangelism will prove to be both instructive and a blessing to all who read it."

—Rev. and Dr. Jerry Mitchell

"I've had the pleasure of knowing Dave Chapman since 2005, and I can attest to his passion for evangelism. His articles on the topic have been included on our JO App, which has been used by 500,000 people to date. He also inspired the development of *The Gift of Heaven* video which reaches millions of people every year with the gospel. Dave's knowledge and experience related to evangelism makes what he writes valuable and practical for anyone involved in ministry."

—Helmut Teichert,
Executive Director, JesusOnline Ministries

"Dave Chapman lives and breathes evangelism. He and Action International Ministries have partnered together for more than a decade including up to a million tracts printed in English and also distributed in Spanish in Cuba and elsewhere. Hundreds of thousands of his tracts have ministered to numerous prisoners throughout the US, Mexico and Central America. In the US, many tracts have been distributed by teams at parks, door-to-door at apartment complexes including to the homeless, refugees or through other personal outreach."

—Bill Flansburg
ACTION Missionary Distributing Publications

"Dave Chapman was on the staff of CRU while I was a student at Portland State University, and we would often share the gospel with students on campus. He would find me on campus and say, 'Hey Jim, what are you doing? Let's go witnessing.' That began a life-long adventure in sharing the gospel in five ministries for over forty years. Dave's the real deal when it comes to turning the good news into great news for people and changing the trajectory of their lives. I've seen the miracle of the new birth happen in others. I'm still doing it and teaching evangelism in my church."

—Jim Wright, PhD
Staff with World Hope Ministries Int'l

"When Dave Chapman speaks or writes, I pay attention. He is an exemplary practitioner of evangelism and disciple-making. Dave eats, drinks, and sleeps the gospel. He rarely, if ever, misses an opportunity to share his faith in Christ. I praise God for Dave's life, ministry, and witness. *Extraordinary Evangelism* will equip the church for years to come."

—Keith R. Krell, PhD
Senior Pastor, Crossroads Bible Church,
Bellevue, WA

"I first knew Dave years ago while sharing the Gospel on the campus of UCLA as I was the Campus Director at the time. I have known him as a man who has been involved intimately with evangelism. His deep-felt desire has been to find ways to share his faith personally. During these years, he has equipped others to be involved in reaching a world in need of Jesus Christ, first on a college campus and then through the local church."

—Dwayne Northrop,
Retired Pastor and Teacher

EXTRAORDINARY EVANGELISM

Equipping You to Reach Your World for Christ

DAVE R. CHAPMAN

LUCIDBOOKS

Extraordinary Evangelism:
Equipping You to Reach Your World for Christ

Copyright © 2024 by Dave R. Chapman
Published by Lucid Books in Houston, TX
www.LucidBooks.com

ISBN: 978-1-63296-683-4

eISBN: 978-1-63296-684-1

Special Sales: Most Lucid Books titles are available in special quantity discounts. Custom imprinting or excerpting can also be done to fit special needs. Contact Lucid Books at Info@LucidBooks.com

To the countless Christians who faithfully and boldly proclaim the gospel even in the face of relentless persecution. They share Christ out of faithful obedience to the Savior because He has changed their lives, and He alone offers the only hope that changes a person's life for all eternity.

To my wife, Bonnie, who has been an amazing blessing and faithful encourager to me as well as to my children. She has tirelessly encouraged me to write this book.

To my brother who has set the example of being in non-vocational ministry and yet has reached millions of people with the gospel.

To Helmut Teichert, the Director of JesusOnline Ministries, who encouraged me and has given me ideas on how to use this material internationally.

To my friend David Schilling who has been extremely helpful with ideas and suggestions for editing and organizing the content.

CONTENTS

INTRODUCTION

My Story

During my senior year in high school, I was dating the prettiest girl on campus. I thought the way to succeed in life and be happy was to marry a beautiful girl. When I met Bonnie, I thought she would fulfill my goal, but after dating her for a year and a half, I sensed there was still something missing in my life. My brother, twin sister, and older sister who had all become Christians were exhibiting a real sense of joy and peace in their lives. I surmised that it wasn't necessarily church that changed their lives. It must have been the Bible because they were reading it often. So, I decided to start reading the Bible, thinking it may have the answers to my search for purpose and contentment in life.

At the time, there was a worldwide threat of nuclear war due to the Cuban Missile Crisis. Our country was on high alert, and most people feared a global nuclear exchange. Nikita Khrushchev, Premier of the Soviet Union during the crisis, said, "we will bury you and the living would envy the dead," if there was a nuclear exchange. I began to wonder what would happen to me if there was ever a nuclear war. Would I live, or would I die? If I lived, I would probably suffer a lot, but if I died, I would go to hell based on Jesus's words in Matthew 5:48: "Therefore you are to be perfect, as your heavenly Father is perfect."

This verse greatly troubled me because I knew God would be my judge someday. The Holy Spirit convicted me of my sin (John 16:8), and shortly after, I got on my knees in the privacy of my room, and not really knowing how to pray, I asked the Lord to forgive me and make me part of His forever family.

When I got up from my knees, I was a changed person. God's Word then became a living, dynamic book. By God's grace, Bonnie became a Christian about a week later as she too was on a quest to understand the Bible at the same time I was. God is good!

A New Mission

I now had a new mission and zeal to reach the lost for Christ, but I did not know how to witness. As a new believer, I knew I would be a lot more effective in witnessing if I got trained in evangelism. I attended a LIFE (Lay Institute for Evangelism) training by Campus Crusade for Christ (now Cru) and was challenged to give my life and career to reach others for Christ.

My wife and I soon joined the Campus Crusade for Christ staff. I had the opportunity to share the gospel with hundreds of college students each year on campuses in the Northwest and at UCLA in Southern California. People at our church were investing in us financially, and it was my job and passion to share my faith and equip believers to share theirs. By nature, I am an introvert, but over time, I learned to be an extrovert. The more I shared the gospel, the easier it became. The best way to learn how to share Christ is simply by doing it.

What's Your Passion?

Elon Musk, founder of Space X and Tesla, has a relentless passion to colonize Mars in order to save humankind in the event of a nuclear war. If you are a Christian, what is your passion? Is it to transform people's lives by sharing the gospel and changing their lives for all eternity? We serve an awesome God who is able to do that through you.

We All Evangelize

We all share our passions about things such as our favorite restaurant, recipe, sports team, and more. But those things will all pass away. Why not share—evangelize—about our passion for Jesus Christ? He is the only way to eternal life. There is nothing more important for us to share. That's why the Apostle Paul was so burdened to evangelize that he wrote, "How terrible it would be for me if I did not preach the gospel!" (1 Corinthians 9:16 GNT).

It's easy to think that evangelism is only for gifted people such as Greg Laurie, Lee Strobel, Josh McDowell, Bill Bright, and Luis Palau. But I've learned that anyone with a personal testimony and a clear understanding of the gospel can share their faith. Regardless of your giftedness, personality, or shortcomings, God can use you to share Christ naturally and effectively.

Marching Orders

Sadly, most people have never heard a clear presentation of the gospel. Eighty percent of Christians do not consistently witness for Christ. But as Christians, we have been given marching orders by the Lord of the universe to proclaim the good news with others.

Jesus said to His disciples, "Thus it is written, that the Christ should suffer and on the third day rise from the dead, and that repentance for the forgiveness of sins should be proclaimed in his name to all nations, beginning from Jerusalem. You are witnesses of these things" (Luke 24:46–48 ESV).

Jesus's final words to every believer are what we call His Great Commission: "Go into all the world and proclaim the gospel to the whole creation" (Mark 16:15 ESV).

Remember, evangelism is for each of us, regardless of our talent, personality, giftedness, or occupation. Former author and theologian D. Elton Trueblood put it clearly. "Evangelism is not a professional job for a few trained men but is instead the unrelenting responsibility of every person who belongs to the company of Jesus."

The purpose of this book is to show you how you can effectively share the gospel to one person at a time and potentially to many people even worldwide. To begin, ask God to help you reach others for Him. He is the One who has promised to help you by His indwelling Holy Spirit.

On the following pages, you'll see how believers and churches are sharing the good news and how the Internet and social media are reaching our world today. But none of these are substitutes for personal evangelism.

There is no greater joy than to see God change a life. Whether you are an extrovert or an introvert, whether you have the gift of gab or not, God can use you. You don't need to have a perfect gospel presentation for the Holy Spirit to reach someone through your testimony and by sharing the gospel. As you apply some of the principles in this book, may the Lord bless you mightily in this grand adventure of sharing the greatest news ever given to all people.

1

OUR MESSAGE

On January 2, 2023, in a Monday night football playoff game between the Buffalo Bills and the Cincinnati Bengals, 24-year-old Damar Hamlin collapsed on the field after being tackled by a Bengals wide receiver. Prayers around the globe went up as Damar hung in the balance between life and death. Ski Mydynski, a senior engineer whose team had developed the best automated external defibrillator (AED) at the time, commented.

> In cases like this of sudden cardiac arrest when one's heart goes into ventricular fibrillation, the only way to save a person's life is to have an AED available and used within the first 10 minutes to save the person's life. Damar was unconscious from no blood flow, and it was

only through the efforts of others that knew he was in trouble that his life was saved. It's similar to believers in Christ who reach out to their non-Christian friends and bring the good news of Jesus through the gospel to save individuals from eternal damnation even if they don't even know it. The person who is about to meet their maker is like someone collapsing from sudden cardiac arrest, the person bringing the good news of the gospel is like a person bringing a life-saving AED to their side. The delivery of the shock is like the Holy Spirit entering someone's life and cleansing them of all their sin once they have chosen to follow Him. The Lord has chosen to use individuals to bring the life-saving message of Jesus Christ to those who are lost.

What Is Evangelism?

Evangelism is believers telling people about God's love for them in Jesus Christ. Luke 2:10 says, "Behold I bring you good news of great joy, which will be for all the people." The Greek word for "good news" is *euangelion* (eu=good; angelion=news). The gospel is literally good news. In ancient war times, a distance runner brought messages from a far-off battle to a city to let the residents know what was happening. The runners were called evangelists—"those who bring good news."

Matthew 4:23 (NKJV) says, "Jesus went about all Galilee, . . . preaching the gospel of the kingdom." The gospel encompasses the life, death, and resurrection of Jesus Christ.

Every Christian is called to be a witness for Christ. First John 1:1 (ESV) says, "That which was from the beginning, which we have heard, which we have seen with our eyes, which we have looked at and our hands have touched—this we proclaim concerning the Word of life."

Romans 1:16 (ESV) says, "For I am not ashamed of the gospel, for it is the power of God for salvation to everyone who believes, to the Jew first and also to the Greek."

The gospel contains both good news and bad news. We short-circuit the gospel when we tell only the good news or only the bad news. We must tell both.

What Is the Bad News?

A doctor tells a patient in the hospital, "We got your test results back, and I have bad news and very bad news." The patient replies, "Oh no! Tell me, please." The doctor replies, "The bad news is you have about 24 hours to live. The very bad news is that I was supposed to tell you yesterday."

What is the "bad news" of the gospel? It's that we've all fallen short of God's moral standards. Romans 3:23 (ESV) says, "For all have sinned and fall short of the glory of God." The word for "sin" is this Greek word ἁμαρτία. It's also an archery term for when someone doesn't hit the target—or more simply, misses the mark. Sin means to fall short of the mark—God's standard of perfection. Ephesians 2:1–3 says that everyone without Christ is dead in their transgressions and deserving of God's wrath.

James 2:10 (ESV) says, "For whoever keeps the whole law but fails in one point has become guilty of all of it."

When I hike and talk to a hiker on the trail, I often turn the conversation to spiritual matters and ask, "Suppose you hiked up Mount Everest and used a chain instead of a rope. If each link represented a commandment of God, how many links would have to break in order for you to fall?" Their answer is always "one." Just one sin in thought, word, or deed is enough to disqualify a person from heaven. The only person who has ever lived a perfect, sinless life is Jesus who died a perfect death on our behalf.

The Coffin Corner

In the early 1980s, National Football League (NFL) punters often kicked the ball to the end of the opponent's end zone—called the "coffin corner"—to pin the opponent inside the one-yard line and make it very difficult for the opposing team to score a touchdown. In evangelism, kicking the ball to the "coffin corner" means getting people to see they have sinned before a holy God and that there are consequences for their sins. Here are some of the many verses in Scripture that show people have sinned before God.

> Romans 3:10—"There is none righteous, not even one."

> Romans 3:23—"For all have sinned and fall short of the glory of God."

> James 2:10—"For whoever keeps the whole law and yet stumbles in one point, he has become guilty of all."

> James 4:17– "Therefore, to the one who knows the right thing to do and does not do it, to him it is sin."

> Matthew 5:48—"Therefore you are to be perfect, as your heavenly Father is perfect."

Most people believe they are essentially good. A 2003 Barna survey showed that most Americans do not expect to experience hell first-hand, and just half of 1 percent expect to go to hell upon their death.

Jesus spoke a lot about heaven, but He also spoke a great deal about hell.

Greg Laurie of Harvest Ministries said, "To promise Heaven and not warn of Hell is to offer forgiveness without repentance." If people reject our message, we need to warn them (Revelation 20:15).

Matthew 25:41 says that hell was made for the devil and his angels. In a real sense, God does not send people to hell. People choose to go to hell by ignoring or rejecting God and His amazing offer of forgiveness.

Repentance and Faith

People need to admit they have sinned and desire to turn from their sins to God. Acts 3:19 (ESV) says, "Repent therefore, and turn back, that your sins may be blotted out." Mark 1:15 (ESV) says, "Jesus came into Galilee, proclaiming the gospel of God, and saying, 'repent and believe in the gospel.'"

Repentance involves turning away from your sin and in faith turning to God for forgiveness with a sincere desire to follow the Lord.

The Amazing Good News

There's the bad news of the gospel, but there's also the incredibly good news. I sometimes ask people if they know what the most famous verse in the Bible is.

A few people say John 3:16, but only a few can quote it. I ask them if they know what it means. It's the gospel in a nutshell. "For God so loved the world, that he gave his only Son, that whoever believes in him should not perish but have eternal life" (John 3:16 ESV). The infinite God-Man Jesus Christ loved us so much that He came to earth to die a horrible, painful death on the cross so we could have the opportunity to spend eternity with Him. The Apostle Paul summed it up well in Galatians 2:20 (ESV) where he said Jesus "loved me and gave Himself for me." Romans 5:8 (ESV) says, "But God shows his love for us in that while we were still sinners, Christ died for us."

God offers us amazing grace! An acronym for grace is **G**od's **R**iches **a**t **C**hrist's **E**xpense. We deserve judgment. We deserve hell. But Jesus in His infinite love and mercy paid our sins' debt by dying on the cross in our place. We are able to leave the courtroom of God's judgment and receive His offer of eternal life by faith.

John MacArthur, pastor of Grace Community Church in Sun Valley, California, said the greatest verse in the Bible on the gospel is 2 Corinthians 5:21, which says, "He made Him who knew no sin to be sin on our behalf, so that we might become the righteousness of God in Him." Jesus bore the punishment we deserve. Our sin and guilt were charged to Christ, and through faith, Christ's righteousness is credited to us. Now we can stand before God sinless, just as Jesus is sinless. Martin Luther called this the Great Exchange.

Christianity is based on the word **DONE**. Jesus paid the full price for our sins. When a person receives God's grace, they are changing their default destination from hell to heaven. The thief, who was dying on a cross next to Jesus, asked Him, "Jesus, remember me when You come into Your kingdom" (Luke 23:42). The thief repented of his sin, received the free gift of eternal life, and became a trophy of God's grace.

Ask the Lord for divine opportunities to share the good news today. Author Lee Strobel in his book *The Unexpected Adventure* wrote, "God might take this seemingly routine day and surprise me with an opportunity to tell someone about the good news that has the power to turn their life inside out. . . . Our role is this: to be ready and willing—because God is always able."

Second Corinthians 6:2 says, "Behold, now is the accepted time; behold, now is the day of salvation." The last breath a person takes may be the last breath God permits them to have.

When someone comes to Christ in God's timing, we're snatching people out of the fire. Jude 23 says, "Save others, snatching them out of the fire."

Always Be Ready

Second Timothy 4:2 (ESV) says, "Preach the word; be ready in season, out of season."

While I was the Pastor of Evangelism at a large church, a fellow pastor mentioned that while his wife was standing in line to get her driver's license, she was talking to a woman who was a sales rep for a cosmetics company. The rep had a rule that every time she was within three feet of a person, she would talk about cosmetics. How much more do we as believers in Christ need to look for opportunities to talk about the good news.

Bill Bright, former president of Campus Crusade for Christ whose ministry has impacted hundreds of millions for Christ, made it a policy that when he was with someone for two to five minutes, he always shared the gospel. Jesus was on a mission to populate heaven. "For the son of man is come to seek and to save that which was lost" (Luke 19:10 (ESV). Acts 1:8 (ESV) says, "You will be my witnesses in Jerusalem and in all Judea and Samaria, and to the end of the earth." That includes our family, our coworkers, our neighbors, and everyone.

2

WHY WITNESS?

*If there was a law against sharing your faith,
would there be enough evidence to convict you?*

Here are several reasons we should witness for Christ.

Our Mandate

Jesus commanded believers to proclaim the gospel. This command is found in all four Gospels and in the book of Acts. Prior to His ascension to heaven, Jesus told His disciples, "All authority has been given to Me in heaven and on earth. Go therefore and make disciples of all the nations, baptizing them in the name of the Father and of the Son and of the Holy Spirit, teaching them to observe all things that I have commanded you; and lo, I am with you always, even to the end of the age" (Matthew 28:18–20). The Great Commission assumes evangelism.

Let's not forget that the Creator of the universe, the One who has infinite authority, has given us a direct command. Pastor Charles Swindoll once said, "Whatever we do, we must not treat the Great Commission like it's the Great Suggestion." Hudson Taylor, British missionary to China, stated, "The Great Commission is not an option to be considered; it is a command to be obeyed."

During the Vietnam War and ten days after I graduated from college, I was caught off guard when I received my induction notice into the U.S. Army. The notice read, "From the President of the United States: Greeting: You are hereby ordered for induction into the Armed Forces of the United States." Our first child was a beautiful daughter of five months old at the time, but I had no choice but to obey the President's command to go into the military and follow his orders, even if it meant dying on the battlefield. I learned how to use an M-16 rifle and machine guns. I learned how to throw grenades and fight hand-to-hand combat.

We are engaged in a cosmic battle, and our Commanding Officer has commissioned us to communicate His good news to as many people as possible. Unfortunately, a lot of Christians go AWOL (absent without leave) or missing in action (MIA) when it comes to the Great Commission.

Evangelist Luis Palau recalled that when he was a new believer, his mother encouraged him to preach the gospel in nearby towns. She said to Luis, "Go, go, go. Get out and reach people with the gospel." Luis told his mother, "Mom, I'm waiting for the call." She got upset with Luis and said, "Luis, the call? The call? The call went out two thousand years ago, Luis! The Lord's waiting for your answer!"

Jesus was the supreme evangelist who set the example for us. "For the Son of Man has come to seek and to save that which was lost" (Luke 19:10).

Practice Makes Perfect

Most Christians fail to witness because they have not been trained to share their faith, they don't think it is their spiritual gift, or they are simply too busy. Evangelism is a spiritual discipline. The more you do evangelism, the more natural it becomes. The Apostle Paul told young Timothy, "But you, be sober in all things, endure hardship, do the work of an evangelist, fulfill your ministry" (2 Timothy 4:5). Evangelist Bill Fay says, "Even if you share stupidly, unlovingly, or with poor timing, our heavenly Father can use it. What He can't use is your silence."

A Guaranteed Harvest

Jesus said, "Don't you have a saying, 'It's still four months until harvest'? I tell you, open your eyes and look at the fields! They are ripe for harvest" (John 4:35 NIV). "Therefore, pray earnestly to the Lord of the harvest to send out laborers into his harvest" (Matthew 9:38 ESV). God is responsible for the harvest; the laborers are to faithfully labor in the harvest.

Jesus told His disciples, "Follow Me, and I will make you fishers of men" (Matthew 4:19 ESV). If we are truly following Christ, we should share the gospel.

Unfortunately, few Christians fail to take the Great Commission seriously. Thom S. Rainer in his book *Sharing the Gospel with Ease* writes, "Based on surveys we've taken . . . fewer than one in twenty Christians have ever had a gospel conversation with someone."

The gospel changes people's lives. I read about Little Richard who bragged about being omnisexual with a diverse lifestyle of sexual promiscuity and drugs, but in 1957, he gave his life to Christ, and Jesus radically changed his life. It's easy to write people off when we think they will never give their life to Christ, but the Lord is in the business of changing people's lives.

In the book of Jonah in the Old Testament, the Lord told Jonah to go preach to the Ninevites, but instead Jonah headed in the exact opposite direction.

Jonah decided to flee God's presence because he detested the Ninevites and did not want to see them turn from their sinful lifestyles. Who would have thought that a wicked city like Nineveh would repent and turn from their evil ways (Jonah 3:10)? It took Jonah being swallowed by a great fish and spending three days inside its belly to get Jonah's attention. In Jonah's outrage, God reminded Jonah, "Should I not have compassion on Nineveh, the great city in which there are more than 120,000 persons who do not know the difference between their right and left hand . . . ?" By God's grace, we are not swallowed by a great fish every time we choose not to share our faith. But as the Lord has compassion on us, we must ask ourselves, "Shouldn't we have compassion on those who don't know Christ who without Him are hopeless and are faced with a Christless eternity?"

Motivated by Love

For the love of Christ controls us, because we have concluded this: that one has died for all, therefore all have died; and he died for all, that those who live might no longer live for themselves but for him who for their sake died and was raised.

—2 Corinthians 5:14–15 ESV

Ask yourself two questions: What's the greatest thing that has happened to you? What's the greatest thing you can do for someone else?

"Therefore, knowing the fear of the Lord, we persuade others" (2 Corinthians 5:11 ESV). Paul's reverential awe for Christ motivated him to keep sharing the gospel of salvation to people in order to receive Christ's commendation at the bema seat of Christ.

In October 2008, the story was reported of the sudden sinking of the cod fishing vessel *Katmai* in the Bering Sea. Something in the stern of the ship went wrong, and experts believe the ship sank in a matter of minutes, giving little opportunity for the crew to prepare to abandon ship. Four men found in a life raft were lifted into a U.S. Coast Guard Jayhawk helicopter. In reasonably good health, the four men insisted that they not return to land but become part of the rescue operation for the others who were still lost at sea. Saved and safe, they insisted that they go after the others. What a clear picture that we who are safe and secure in the grip of God's grace have the urgent call to go after others who are still lost.

We're Ambassadors for Christ

The Britannica Dictionary defines an ambassador as "the highest-ranking person who represents his or her own government while living in another country." As Christians, we are citizens of heaven who represent the King of kings and Lord of lords as official representatives to carry the good news of the King—the gospel—to those on earth. As ambassadors for Christ, we are given the ministry of reconciliation (2 Corinthians 5:18–20). It's not so much if you are a witness but rather what type of witness you are.

People Are Lost Without Christ

Jesus said to Thomas, "I am the way, and the truth, and the life. No one comes to the Father except through me" (John 14:6 ESV). "And there is salvation in no one else, for there is no other name under heaven given among men by which we must be saved" (Acts 4:12 ESV).

When I have shared Christ with people and asked them if they have ever heard the gospel before, 90 percent or more of them have said no.

Pastor and author David Jeremiah said, "If we understand what lies ahead for those who do not know Christ, there will be a sense of urgency in our witness."

While in seminary, I was an intern for a period of time at the USC Medical Hospital under Chaplain Phil Manly. One day, a young man was brought into the burn ward with severe third-degree burns over

95 percent of his body after his apartment caught on fire. He was in excruciating pain. I visited him several times and tried to share the gospel, but he was barely conscious. After a month of agony, his body finally gave out. I don't know if he ever asked the Lord for forgiveness, but I trust that in his dying, agonizing moments, he responded in faith. In Luke 16:19–31, Jesus tells the story of the rich man and Lazarus who was poor. Both died, and the rich man who ended up in hell said, "'Father Abraham, have mercy on me . . . for I am tormented in this flame'" (Luke 16:24).

In the movie *Gladiator*, Russell Crowe as the Roman General Maximus addresses his troops before battle. He tells them, "What we do in life . . . echoes in eternity."

Second Peter 3:9 says that God is longsuffering toward us, not willing that any should perish but that all should come to repentance. Second Corinthians 2:15–16 says, "For we are a fragrance of Christ to God among those who are being saved and among those who are perishing; to the one an aroma of death to death, to the other an aroma from life to life."

Atheist Penn Jillette of the magician duo Penn & Teller said, "How much do you have to hate somebody to believe everlasting life is possible and not tell them that? I mean, if I believed, beyond the shadow of a doubt, that a truck was coming at you, and you didn't believe that truck was bearing down on you, there is a certain point where I tackle you. And this is *more* important than that." Tragically, he is still an atheist who is basically saying if the gospel is true, we should go all out to tell others about the truth.

Suppose you discovered a cure for cancer and didn't tell anyone. You would be considered totally self-centered if you did not share that great discovery with others. Billy Graham said, "If we really believe that men are lost apart from Jesus Christ, it should become a burning incentive to evangelize with zeal and passion." Dwight L. Moody said, "I cannot preach on hell unless I preach with tears."

Here are the two great motivators for sharing Christ: (1) the amazing offer and glorious promise of heaven for those who trust Jesus for their salvation and (2) the dire warnings of hell for those who ignore God and for whatever reason reject God's offer of love and forgiveness.

We Will be Rewarded for Our Witness for Christ

And those who are wise shall shine like the brightness of the sky above; and those who turn many to righteousness, like the stars forever and ever.

—Daniel 12:3 ESV

For what is our hope or joy or crown of boasting before our Lord Jesus at his coming? Is it not you? For you are our glory and joy.

—1 Thessalonians 2:19–20 ESV

God's plan for enlarging His kingdom is . . . one person telling another about the Savior. . . . The joy you'll have when you meet that person in heaven will far exceed any discomfort you felt in sharing the gospel.

—Charles Stanley

I never regret sharing Christ with others. I only regret it when I don't share Christ with someone I should have. Chuck Swindoll said, "Your courage to acknowledge Jesus publicly will be rewarded." Your willingness to accept rejection even from family members (Matthew 10:32–36) will be rewarded.

Recently, I hiked up a famous trail in Washington state called Mount Si. At the top of the climb, I shared Christ with three hikers in their early 30s. After I shared the gospel with them, one of the young hikers said in the presence of his other buddies, "I did that." He meant he had previously received Christ and was a citizen of heaven. His other two hiking buddies were listening to what he said. I thought to myself, *Thank you, Lord, for letting me finally get to the top with this weighed pack and share Christ with these three hikers.*

Hopefully, his other two friends were impacted by his testimony.

The Lord can use you right where you are. My brother Larry at 16 years of age was led to Christ by an anesthesiologist we called Doc. He was the high school football team's doctor. Several years later, my brother, as a layman, had reached millions of people for Christ through his ministry called Jesusonlineministries.com. Little did Doc know that this 16-year-old high school kid would impact millions for the gospel.

Time Is Short

Evangelist Mark Cahill wrote a book called *One Thing You Can't Do in Heaven*—and that one thing is that there will be no witnessing since the lost won't be there. Jesus said in John 9:4 (ESV) that "night is coming when no one can work."

The Lord's coming is getting closer every day. Think of all the people you work with, your neighbors, and those you see on the street, at the park, at the gym, and in the supermarket. The old saying holds true: "As death finds you, eternity keeps you." We should have a sense of urgency as we witness for Christ because life is short.

Dennis was a guy from church I would occasionally go witnessing with until one day he fell 100 feet to his death on a solo hike. Dennis can no longer witness because he is now in heaven. None of us knows how many hours, days, minutes, or seconds we have left on earth.

A friend of mine, Gerry Autry who worked for Youth for Christ, told me a story of a girl named Dawn who went to a junior high retreat, got motivated to share her faith, and went back home and shared Christ with a friend who received Christ. Six hours later, that friend was raped and killed. She is now in heaven forever.

Psalm 90:12 says, "So teach us to number our days, that we may present to You a heart of wisdom." If you had one week to live, what would you do? Would you be focused on reaching your unsaved loved ones, friends, and coworkers for Christ?

Chuck Swindoll in his commentary on the Gospel of Luke wrote, "This may be your last day to choose, because there is not only a heaven, and there is not only a hell; there is a hurry."

John Harper's Last Convert

John Harper was an evangelist who was invited to speak at The Moody Church in 1910. He had been invited to speak to The Moody Church for three months of meetings.

John Harper, his sister, and his six-year-old

daughter (his wife had died) found themselves on the great ship, the *Titanic*. Survivors later reported that as *Titanic* began to sink, Harper admonished people to be prepared to die. He made sure his sister and daughter were in a lifeboat even as he continued to share the Gospel with whoever would listen. And when he found himself in the icy water with a life jacket, floating near another man, Harper asked, "Are you saved?" "No, I'm not saved!" the desperate man replied. "Believe on the Lord Jesus Christ and you will be saved!" Harper shouted.

Harper knew that he could not survive in the icy water. He took off his life jacket and threw it to another person with the words, "You need this more than I do!" Moments later, Harper disappeared beneath the water. Four years later, when there was a reunion of the survivors of the *Titanic,* the man to whom Harper had witnessed told the story of his rescue and gave a testimony of his conversion recorded in a tract, *I was John Harper's Last Convert.* The Gospel does not spare us from drowning in an ocean, but it does spare us from a far worse eternal destruction.

In Matthew 24:14 (NKJV), Jesus says, "This gospel of the kingdom will be preached in all the world as a witness to all the nations, and then the end will come."

The Lord is delaying His return to give more

people an opportunity to come to Christ before He returns to set up His kingdom.

Ask the Lord to give you an open door to share His good news with others. Ask yourself, "Who in my life needs Jesus?" List the names of five to seven people you know who don't know Christ, and then pray about how to share the gospel with them. It starts with prayer and then a follow-up plan of some kind such as a letter, a phone call, an invitation to church, a book, or doing something together.

3

WHO TO SHARE CHRIST WITH

But you will receive power when the Holy Spirit has come upon you, and you will be my witnesses in Jerusalem and in all Judea and Samaria, and to the end of the earth.

—Acts 1:8 ESV

"Jerusalem" refers to those who are closest to you—family, coworkers, neighbors, people you hang out with. "All Judea and Samaria" refers to your acquaintances or people you may only talk to once on an airplane, in a coffee shop, at the grocery store, at a sporting event, or on an Uber ride. Those at "the end of the earth" might be someone overseas you talk to on the phone, email, or conference call.

Sharing Christ with Family

My Mother

My mother was raised in a typical churchgoing home with godly parents who were farmers in Pennsylvania. Although she believed in Jesus and prayed to God, she never showed any evidence of a real conversion.

When I was 11 years old, my brother became a Christian through the ministry of Young Life. Soon after, my sisters Ann and Donna also gave their lives to Christ. As their lives all began to change, God stirred my heart, and I realized the need to surrender my life to Christ like they had done. I began to have a burden for my mother, and one day I shared my personal testimony with her about how Christ changed my life. I had never seen my mom read the Bible and mentioned my concern to her. She sincerely remarked, "Well, maybe I'm not a Christian." She was not offended by my question, but I think it was something she had thought about from time to time.

My mom often attended a strong, Bible-believing church in Southern California and enjoyed the sermons. After my father died, she became close friends with a man named Jus Moyer who wasn't a believer. Several years after they met, Jus got stage-four cancer, and Pastor Dick Jeffers led him to Christ. Suddenly, Jus was full of hope and joy, which greatly affected my mother. Shortly after Jus died, my mom gave her life to Christ. When I asked her what happened, she remarked, "I had a head knowledge of Christ but not a heart knowledge." Mom began reading God's Word and books about the Bible. Her life completely changed. To me, that was evidence of the new birth. "Therefore, if anyone is in Christ, he is a new creation. The old has passed away; behold, the new has come" (2 Corinthians 5:17 ESV).

It's easy to assume that people who have been raised in a strong, biblical church are Christians, but that is not always the case. Once I witnessed to a lady in her 60s who has been a Southern Baptist all of her life. When I asked what she would say to God if He asked, "Why should I let you into heaven?" she replied, "I believe in letting your conscience be your guide." Even though she had gone to church all her life, she showed no evidence that she knew Christ personally. You may have heard the old saying: "Going to church doesn't make you a Christian any more than going into a garage makes you a car."

Jesus told Nicodemus in John 3:8, "The wind blows where it wishes and you hear the sound of it, but do not know where it comes from or where it is going; so is everyone who is born of the Spirit." Salvation can be likened to the wind. The wind is unseen and mysterious, but we see its effects. In the same way, someone who is born again is a new creation, and the result is a changed life. Ultimately, the Holy Spirit is the One who turns the switch on in a person's life from being dead spiritually to being made alive spiritually unto God. That is what happened to my mother.

My Son-in Law

When my daughter Christy was a senior in high school, she started dating a guy who was not a Christian. My wife and I bathed our daughter in prayer because she was dating a non-Christian. Near the end of Christy's college education, she broke up with him after they had been dating three years. Christy met another non-Christian guy named Steve, and although Christy liked Steve a lot, she made it clear to him that he needed to go to church with her and make Christ the center of their relationship since she did not want to get involved in another relationship with a non-Christian.

Christy introduced us to Steve and asked if I could talk with him about the Lord. Steve's parents got divorced when Steve was very young, and his only exposure to religion was when he randomly went to church with his family and attended Catholic schools. Because Steve took a strong liking to our daughter, he was very open when I invited him to have breakfast with me for the purpose of sharing the gospel with him. During that breakfast, I simply asked Steve if he thought he was going to heaven. His answer was typical for a non-believer: "I think so." Then I asked him why God would let him in. Steve said it was because he was "a pretty good person and hadn't killed anyone."

I showed Steve Ephesians 2:8–9, which says, "For by grace you have been saved through faith; and that not of yourselves, it is the gift of God; not as a result of works, so that no one may boast." Steve immediately saw that getting to heaven was not by works but by having a personal relationship with Jesus Christ. After sharing the gospel with Steve, he received Christ into his life as his Lord and Savior. Steve and Christy soon began attending a dynamic, Bible-believing church, and Steve quickly grew in his faith.

Eventually they got married and moved to Arizona where Steve was mentored by the leader of a men's ministry at a large, Bible-believing church. Since then, Steve has been actively involved in men's Bible studies, discipling, leading men in their relationship with Jesus, and modeling a commitment to Christ to Christy and their two sons. We are truly blessed to have Steve as part of our family.

Sometimes those closest to us are the hardest to share Christ with. In Mark 6:4 (NIV), Jesus said to His disciples, "A prophet is not without honor except in his own town, among his relatives and in his own home." If Jesus was rejected by his own family early on, don't be surprised if sharing Christ with your family can be challenging and often takes time.

My Father

I was raised in a family who believed in Jesus superficially. Early on in my life, before I was a Christian, my father woke up our family very early on Easter Sunday to go to the Hollywood Bowl in Southern California for a 6:00 a.m. service. My father did that out of tradition even though he was not a Christian at the time. He had gone to Sunday school as a child when he visited his godly grandparents. Dad even taught us John 3:16, and during our Sunday meals he would have us all say the Lord's Prayer together. However, as Dad began drinking, he no longer took us to church or talked about Christianity.

During my early teen years, my brother, two sisters, and I had tried to share Christ with our father several times, but he was stubborn and argumentative. As I grew in my faith, I began to have a burden for him. While I was in the military, I wrote a letter to him to let him know I loved him but that I also wanted him to give his life to Christ. He wrote me back and explained why he didn't feel the need to commit himself to Christ. But the Lord was not done getting his attention and breaking his will. Dad had dreamed of taking Mom on a second honeymoon to Europe. In 1971, he was finally able to take her, but while they were driving in Italy, they got in a serious car accident on the Autostrada. Dad ended up with broken ribs, bedridden in an Italian hospital. Mom was injured, too, but was able to visit Dad a couple times each day.

Since Dad's ribs were broken, he was strapped to the bed, unable to move. He couldn't smoke or take a drink. Since he didn't speak Italian, he could only lie there on his back day and night.

After the hospital took Dad off the critical list, he demanded to be released from the hospital. But the nurses told Mom that he had come down with pneumonia. That same evening, as Dad was demanding to be released, Mom told him, "Gene, you can't get out of the hospital because you've got pneumonia."

That news stunned Dad. He had been stricken with pneumonia earlier in his life and had been told to never lie flat on your back if you have pneumonia. Mom said that immediately after Dad heard her words, his face grew pale, and he began breathing heavily. Dad spent the next few hours alone with his thoughts and fears. The next morning, the nurses rushed Mom into Dad's room where she felt his still warm but lifeless body.

It is our hope that God heard Dad's cries that evening as expressed in Psalm 22:24 (TLB): "He has not despised my cries of deep despair; he has not turned and walked away. When I cried to him, he heard and came."

Our family believes by faith that in the waning moments of his life, our father cried out to the Lord in full surrender. Sometimes it takes a tragedy to get our attention, much like the thief on the cross who asked, "Jesus, remember me when You come in Your kingdom" (Luke 23:42), and Jesus graciously replied, "Truly I say to you, today you shall be with Me in Paradise" (Luke 23:43). When I get to heaven, I'll be looking for my father.

My Brother-in-Law

The same was true for my wife's brother Dave. He was voted one of the top 10 teachers in the state of California. He had a type A personality—a perfectionist—and everything he did was full throttle. He flew airplanes, water skied on his bare feet, had a beautiful wife and family, and loved life to the fullest. To satisfy his need for acceptance, however, Dave resorted to alcohol, which eventually became his downfall and resulted in separating from his wife.

While separated, Dave lived for about a year with a neighborhood friend from his childhood. This friend hosted two retired missionary women from China. My wife and these two women shared the gospel with Dave, but he was still addicted to alcohol. My brother-in-law, Bob, befriended Dave and brought about a turning point in Dave's life. Bob is a godly Christian, inventor, and manufacturer who owned a large successful business with hundreds of employees. Dave was attracted to Bob's Christian character and commitment as a successful businessman. They became friends, and during the last few days of Dave's life, Dave prayed with Bob to receive Christ. The next morning, Dave choked on a piece of food during breakfast, and the Lord took him home to heaven. There's an African proverb that says, "It takes a village to raise a child." In a similar way, it can take more than one family member and often many mini steps to impact a person for Christ.

On the other hand, one of my wife's relatives has stubbornly resisted coming to Christ even though he has heard the gospel many times from all members of our family, including the grandkids. Be persistent in prayer. Ask the Holy Spirit to open and soften their hearts. Ask the Lord to let His light shine through you (Matthew 5:16). Offer them books or video clips that might be of interest to them.

A lot is happening now in Israel and the Middle East that is a fulfillment of biblical prophecy. As we approach the end times, the Middle East and Israel will become more of a concern to world leaders and people in general. Here is a good question to ask people: "What concerns you today in the news?" That could be an entry to the gospel as people share their fears of the future. Prayer is the key to reaching family for Christ.

Cru has the following five principles for how to talk about Jesus with loved ones:

1. Lead with vulnerability and brokenness. When we expose our brokenness to others, it helps people see their own need for Christ and His grace.

2. Show an interest in what's important to them. Listening to what people are most concerned about provides entry points for the gospel.

3. Bring them into a community of Jesus followers. Expose them to a group of people who care for one another.

4. Pray with and for your family members. Randy Newman in his book *Bringing the Gospel Home* recommends, "Develop a system for prayer for your family." That includes giving thanks for God's love for each family member and perhaps confession of your lack of love for your family.

5. Be patient. Seeing someone come to Christ takes patience. We are called to water and plant, but it's God who brings growth.

Reaching Friends of Family

When our oldest son, Dan, was around 12 years of age, he became best friends with a kid named Charlie who said, "Dan kept me in line on many occasions." According to Charlie, Dan was a good model of what a Christ-follower looks like. Charlie and Dan often played baseball and basketball together, caught crawdads in the local creek, and occasionally went camping with our family. Charlie watched closely how our family interacted with one another and how my wife treated the family with kindness and unconditional love. That attracted Charlie to our family. It was during this time that Charlie was experiencing some emotional issues and depression in his life. Our family was concerned about Charlie because he was like a son to us. He felt very comfortable around our family, and Dan and Charlie had become like brothers.

One day Charlie was downstairs in our split-level home. I felt he would be willing to hear the gospel. I asked Charlie if I could share the Four Spiritual Laws with him, and he readily agreed. Law Four says, "We must individually receive Jesus Christ as Savior and Lord; then we can know and experience God's love and plan for our lives." At the end of Law Four, I showed Charlie the prayer to receive Christ. He was very open to the gospel and prayed to invite Jesus into his life as his personal Savior and Lord that day. He didn't change overnight, but the seed was planted in his heart. Charlie believes that Dan and our family are the reasons he is a Christian. Years later, Charlie married a pastor's daughter, and he is fully committed to being the spiritual leader of his family. He is a successful nurse anesthesiologist in the greater Seattle area and is passing the baton of the gospel on to his family and others.

Reaching Neighbors

One day I saw a student on the lawn at a local community college between classes. I asked him what he was studying in school. He said he was studying sociology—the study of some of the societal issues facing the world such as poverty, famine, disease, earthquakes, and war. I mentioned that some of those issues related to Bible prophecy, and that caught his interest. He could see the correlation between what he was studying in school and what the Bible said. I asked him if I could share how to have a personal relationship with God. He was very open to that.

One of the keys to sharing Christ is to find out what concerns people today or what interests they have and then relate it to the gospel. Some people are interested in sports, and there are many athletes, especially in pro football, who are committed to Christ.

Many people today are fearful of the future, inflation, the prospect of nuclear war, and national security. Find out what people are concerned about or what interests them, and then try to use it as a bridge to the gospel.

One of our next-door neighbors was a family of five. The wife and husband frequently yelled, argued, and got into physical altercations that ultimately ended in divorce. Our three sons often played with their three sons. We invited Brandon, the oldest son, to our church, and years later after he became a Christian, he said he had felt insecure going to church because his family never went. I had witnessed to him, but he was not ready to receive Christ at the time. When Brandon was 13 years old, his family moved away, and he met a young lady who was a pastor's daughter. She told him, "You can hang out with me as long as you go to my church." Brandon agreed and soon committed his life to Christ. They are now married and have three children. One of our sons apologized to Brandon for not verbally sharing the gospel with him. But Brandon graciously told us, "Your family planted seeds in my garden."

Recently, two couples moved into our neighborhood. One is a young, newly married couple. The other family is from India; they have two children. There is also a third family in our neighborhood—a single mom from India with two children. We decided to host a dessert at our home with all three families, and it went very well. Our goal was to build relationships with our neighbors over time and then see how we could eventually in God's time introduce Christ to them. Recently we let one of those families use our home while we were visiting our children for Thanksgiving in another state. Our hope and prayer was that they would see the "music of the gospel" like Joel Aldrich said in his book *Lifestyle Evangelism* and then share Christ with them when we felt the timing was right.

Sharing Christ with neighbors can be challenging. *The Art of Neighboring* by Jay Pathak and Dave Runyon explains how to build genuine relationships right outside your door. It's based on Luke 10:27, which says, "You shall love the Lord your God with all your heart, and with all your soul, and with all your strength, and with all your mind; and your neighbor as yourself." Their authors' website (https://www.artofneighboring.com) provides stories, tools, and resources for how to reach your neighbors for Christ.

Sharing Christ with People Different Than You

Paul said in 1 Corinthians 9:22, "I have become all things to all men, so that I may by all means save some." We're all equally valued in God's eyes. It may seem easier to share Christ with people who are just like us, but what about those who are totally different than us? No one is too lost, too sinful, too insignificant, too old, too young, or too poor. In Luke 5:31–32 (KJV), Jesus said, "They that are whole need not a physician; but they that are sick. I came not to call the righteous, but sinners to repentance." In the Bible, who do you think were the least likely to repent and believe in Christ? You would be right if you thought it was the Apostle Paul who killed Christians (Acts 8), the man possessed by demons (Mark 5), or the woman caught in adultery (John 8), and yet the Lord reached all of them.

Scott was a young man in his early 20s who had long hair, wore ragged clothes, and often picked up tracts he saw on the ground and read them. The Lord was preparing Scott's heart, and he was intrigued by what he read. I shared the gospel with Scott, and soon after, he wanted to know what the Bible said about the future because some of the tracts he picked up spoke of future events. Scott read a book on prophecy, and shortly after, he received Christ as his Savior. He cut his long hair, went to Multnomah School of the Bible, and gave me the *Thompson Chain Reference Bible* as a gift. Sometimes a simple gospel tract can be the seed in a person's heart to receive Christ later on.

Who in My Life Needs Jesus?

Be available and willing to share Christ with all people, especially those who may have hit bottom with drugs, alcohol, unemployment, sex trafficking, or homelessness. They may be the most open to the Lord because they've hit rock bottom and see their need for a Savior.

Statistics show that when a person becomes a Christian, they lose contact with all unbelieving friends within an average of two years. Jesus saw people as valuable, created in the image of God—people the Father cares about. We are called to be Jesus to our world where people experience guilt and loneliness. Many of them were raised in a broken home, lack purpose, and are overcome with sin and uncertainty about their future.

I once visited a beautiful young lady in the hospital. She had become distraught because her boyfriend had broken up with her, and in her despair, she drank Lysol in an attempt to commit suicide. The Lysol destroyed her stomach lining, but she lived. The Lord reached her as she prayed to receive Christ. Jesus said, "I have come that they may have life, and have it abundantly" (a full and meaningful life) (John 10:10). We have the only answer to their deepest needs. Jesus said in John 14:2 (ESV), "In My Father's house are many rooms . . . I am going to prepare a place for you." God wants to fill His house (heaven) with many people, more than we can count. There's room in God's house if they will respond to Jesus's invitation. Let's move closer to the unbeliever and pray about new ways to reach the lost for Christ.

4

WHY CHRISTIANS DON'T WITNESS

Fear is one of the main reasons people don't witness. I was teaching evangelism at a church, and one of the attendees raised her hand and said, "I agree with what you have said, but how do you get rid of the fear?" I said, "You don't. You need to do evangelism, and then you'll get over some of the fear. But if you have no fear, maybe you aren't trusting the Lord." Aaron Pierce in his book *Not Beyond Reach* wrote, "Fear doesn't disqualify you from being used by God; it simply reminds you of your dependence on Him."

In sports, experts say "muscle memory" is a process that allows your body to remember certain motor skills and perform them without conscious effort. That can be achieved through practice and repetition. The more you share the gospel, the easier it will become.

The Apostles Peter and John were arrested and brought before the Sanhedrin. "Now as they observed the confidence of Peter and John and understood that they were uneducated and untrained men, they were amazed, and began to recognize them as having been with Jesus" (Acts 4:13 NIV). This was their reply before the council: "For we cannot stop speaking about what we have seen and heard" (Acts 4:20 NIV). Even though they were being persecuted, it did not stop them from passionately sharing the gospel.

Persecution Is Not Uncommon

In many countries such as Syria, Iran, Egypt, and Iraq, Muslims who come to Christ often face persecution. These Christians are tortured for their faith and nailed to crosses. In North Korea, Christians are murdered for owning a Bible.

Christianity is increasingly coming under attack in America. High school coach Joe Kennedy was fired for exercising his First Amendment right to pray to God in public. It took him almost seven years to undo this unjust persecution when the Supreme Court finally ruled in his favor.

Tertullian was an early church father and author who wrote, "The blood of the martyrs is the seed of the church." Persecution caused the early church to spread like wildfire. The word *martyr* comes from the

Greek for "witness"—someone who gives testimony. It came to be associated with someone who died because of their testimony for Jesus.

The Apostle Paul was stoned at Lystra and left for dead, but the next day he went with Barnabas to Derbe to preach the gospel. George Barna stated, "As fewer people share our theological and worldview commitments, Christians will need courage that was not required of recent generations of believers."

Every year, some people die trying to climb Mount Rainier in Washington state, which is 14,411 ft. in elevation. Some fall into a crevasse, some have a heart attack, and some even freeze to death. But the dangers do not deter people from climbing. There may be risks in sharing our faith, but there is a great reward. The joy and blessing of sharing our faith should supersede the fear of being persecuted. Jesus said, "If they persecuted Me, they will also persecute you" (John 15:20 ESV). So why do believers fail to witness?

1. Fear of Rejection

Remember that successful witnessing is simply taking the initiative to share Christ in the power of the Holy Spirit and leaving the results with God. The Apostle Paul said, "I came to you in weakness and great fear and trembling. My message and my preaching were not with wise and persuasive words, but with a demonstration of the Spirit's power, so that your faith might not rest on human wisdom, but on God's power" (1 Corinthians 2:3–5 NIV).

Even the great Apostle Paul felt inadequate at times to share the gospel. Moses said to God, "I have never been eloquent. . . . I am slow of speech and slow of tongue" (Exodus 4:10 ESV). God is interested in your availability more than your ability. God can take your inadequacy and make it adequate for Him.

2. Fear of What My Friends Will Think

Bill Fay in his book *Share Jesus without Fear* wrote, "Either you can share your faith, or you can say nothing and . . . love your friends into hell." Most people have never heard the gospel, and many are waiting for you to tell them. Even if they initially reject your message, at some point they may come to faith in Christ.

3. Fear of Losing Friends and Loved Ones

Jesus said our witness for Christ will at times cause division in our families and among our friends. "Do you think I came to bring peace on earth? No, I tell you, but division" (Luke 12:51–53 ESV).

I have never regretted sharing Christ with others. Some came to Christ, and most did not receive the Lord. It can be a lot easier to witness when you are sitting next to someone on an airplane or with someone you meet casually. Our families are familiar with our lives, so we need to pray for the Lord to open their hearts. Remember that the Lord does the saving. Ask the Lord to help you demonstrate the love of Christ to them. Back up your words with godly actions. Share your personal testimony and how Christ changed your life.

Fear of Not Knowing Enough

Fear of not knowing enough usually comes from a believer who has been a Christian for several years. If you don't know the answer to a question, simply state, "That's a good question. Let me research the answer and get back to you on this." Get their contact information, and research the answer on the Internet. Ask an elder or pastor of your church. I recommend memorizing the basics of the gospel tract, so they become second nature to you when you witness. If it is difficult for you to memorize, there are downloadable tracts on your mobile device that clearly present the gospel. The more we are prepared to share our faith, the easier it will be to become a witness for Christ.

When David Livingstone, the great missionary to Africa, returned to his native home in Scotland, his body was emaciated by some 27 fevers during his service. His left arm hung limply by his side; it had been mangled by a lion. As he spoke to the students at Glasgow University, he said, "Shall I tell you what sustained me during the hardship and loneliness of my exile? It was Christ's promise, 'Lo, I am with you always, even to the end of the age.'"

This is the same great promise and motivation to every believer as they share their faith with others. God grants His power (Acts 1:8) and His presence as we tell others about Jesus.

Jesus sent out His disciples "in the midst of wolves" (Matthew 10:16 ESV) to proclaim the gospel to Israel. Three times He told them, "Do not fear" (Matthew 10:26, 28, 31 NKJV). Hebrews 13:5 says, "For He Himself has said, 'I will never desert you, nor will I ever forsake you.'" Jesus promised that He will be with us as we proclaim the gospel.

When all else fails in terms of your not feeling like you know enough to share your faith, you still have your personal testimony. That is a true story, and people like to hear true stories.

5

THE POWER

Power Source #1: The Holy Spirit

Evangelism is about the supernatural work of the Holy Spirit who enables us to share the good news. The Holy Spirit is the One who causes a person to put their faith in Christ. In Acts 1:4, Jesus commanded His disciples to wait for what the Father had promised—to be endued with power from the Holy Spirit. The Lord will never ask us to do something without giving us the resources to do it. Ephesians 5:18 says, "And do not get drunk with wine, for that is dissipation, but be filled with the Spirit."

Paul said in 1 Corinthians 2:4 (NKJV), "My message and preaching was not in persuasive words of wisdom, but in demonstration of the Spirit and of power." Whether you use a tract or simply share the gospel from your heart, you are to rely on the Holy Spirit. God uses ordinary people filled with extraordinary power to share the good news. All glory goes to the Lord when a person comes to Christ.

Bill Bright in his booklet "How You Can Be Filled with the Holy Spirit" explains how important it is to be controlled by the Holy Spirit when we share Christ with others.

It is Christ himself, living within you in all of his resurrection power . . . speaking with your lips—who will empower you with the Holy Spirit. It is not your wisdom, your eloquence, your logic, your good personality, or your persuasiveness that brings people to our Savior. First-century Christians, controlled and empowered by the Holy Spirit and filled with his love, turned the world upside down. As the disciples were filled with the Holy Spirit, they received a divine, supernatural power that changed them from fearful men to radiant witnesses for Christ. They were used by God to change the course of history. And this same omnipotent power, the power of the Holy Spirit, is available to you to enable you to live a . . . fruitful life for Jesus Christ.

Jesus told His disciples that the Holy Spirit "will convict the world concerning sin and righteousness and judgment" (John 16:8 NKJV). The Holy Spirit shows the non-Christian their need for Christ, and unless they repent of sin and accept Jesus as their Savior and refuge, they will face the God's judgment.

Ask the Lord to fill you with the Holy Spirit and show you what steps to take as you share Christ with others, whether they are a neighbor, a relative, a coworker, or a friend.

Power Source #2: Prayer

Someone once said, "When we work, we work, but when we pray, God works." Without prayer, evangelism is impotent. Author E. M. Bounds said, "Prayer is the mightiest agent to advance God's work."

The early church was a model for prayer. They prayed for 10 days and preached for 10 minutes, and 3,000 were saved (Acts 1–2). As Pastor J. D. Greear said, "Nowadays, we pray for 10 minutes, we talk for 10 days, and three people get saved."

Prayer is an act of humility and aligns our hearts with God's heart to open blind eyes and deaf ears to the gospel. What should we pray for?

Pray to Have a Heart for the Lost

Ask the Lord to forgive you for being apathetic toward the lost. Talk to the Lord and say, "Lord, please forgive me, and give me a heart for those who don't know You." Trust God, and step out in faith as you look for divine appointments. Paul told Philemon, "I pray that you may be active in sharing your faith, so that you will have a full understanding of every good thing we have in Christ" (Philemon 6 NIV).

Pray for Boldness

The greatest missionary who ever lived, the Apostle Paul, asked for prayer in Ephesians 6:19: "And pray on my behalf, that utterance may be given to me in the opening of my mouth, to make known with boldness the mystery of the gospel . . . that . . . I may speak boldly, as I ought to speak."

John and Peter said, "Now, Lord, look on their threats, and grant to your servants that with all boldness they may speak your word" (Acts 4:29 NKJV).

When I was on staff with Cru, I was given the assignment of reaching the fraternities for Christ at UCLA. Fraternity life is often filled with sexual promiscuity, drunken behavior, and an anything-goes lifestyle. I prayed for boldness, and my team was able to share the gospel to 10 of the 11 fraternities. I claimed 2 Timothy 1:7 (NKJV) where Paul said, "For

God has not given us a spirit of fear, but of power and of love and of a sound mind."

Ralph Drollinger was on our outreach team to reach the fraternities for Christ. He was a 7'2" basketball player at UCLA, and when we walked into the fraternities, all the frat guys were impressed with his height. They would often walk up to Ralph and ask, "How's the weather up there?" They listened to Ralph and our team as we presented the gospel. Ralph initially turned down a pro basketball contract in order to share Christ with thousands of college and semi pro players while playing basketball for Athletes in Action. Today, he is a ministry leader with Capitol Ministries, leading Bible studies with members of Congress.

Pray for Open Doors and Divine Opportunities

Paul said in Colossians 4:3 (NKJV), "Meanwhile praying also for us, that God would open to us a door for the word." Open doors are divine opportunities bathed in prayer that produce fruit. In Acts 18:9–10 (ESV), the Lord spoke to Paul in a vision, saying, "Do not be afraid; keep on speaking, do not be silent. For I am with you, and no one is going to attack and harm you, because I have many people in this city."

Crossroads Bible Church has this motto: Passionate Prayer. They have a Sunday morning prayer gathering before the first service, an online prayer ministry during both services, prayer after the services at the foot of the cross, corporate prayer on Tuesday evenings, monthly all-church worship and prayer, prayer in community groups, and prayer in the various ministries of the church.

Pray That Spiritual Eyes and Hearts Will Be Open to the Gospel

Ask the Lord that His Word will not return void (Isaiah 55:11). Pray for a person by name that they will understand the gospel.

"And even if our gospel is veiled, it is veiled to those who are perishing, in whose case the god of this world has blinded the minds of the unbelieving so that they might not see the light of the gospel of the glory of Christ, who is the image of God" (2 Corinthians 4:3–4). Satan's main goal is to keep people locked in darkness and take as many people to hell as possible.

Pray that the non-believer will recognize their need for Christ much like the Samaritan woman at the well when she said to Jesus, "Sir, give me this water, that I may not thirst" (John 4:15). Paul said, "Grant them repentance, so that they may know the truth, and . . . come to their senses and escape the snare of the devil" (2 Timothy 2:25–26).

Ask a non-Christian if you can pray for them. That shows compassion. At a restaurant, ask the waitress, "How are things going?" or "How is your day going?" People are often very receptive to being prayed for.

Pastor Kevin Harney in his book *Organic Outreach* suggests keeping the prayer simple when you pray for them. Use common language. Lift up their needs and joys, pray in Jesus's name, and stay in touch. If you see them again, your compassion in praying for them may provide an open door for more spiritual conversations.

Pray That Satan Would Be Hindered from Stealing the Seed of the Gospel

Ephesians 6:10–13 says we are engaged in a spiritual battle. The weapons we fight with are not those of the world. Paul said, "For . . . the weapons of our warfare are not of the flesh, but divinely powerful for the destruction of fortresses" (2 Corinthians 10:3–4).

Satan is on an all-out mission to hinder non-Christians, including your neighbors, your family, and your friends, from receiving Christ. He wants to do everything possible to convince believers that they are inadequate to share their faith.

Jesus said, "When anyone hears the word of the kingdom and does not understand, the evil one comes and snatches away what has been sown in his heart" (Matthew 13:19). As believers, we have the power of prayer, the Holy Spirit, and the Word of God to advance God's kingdom and tear down strongholds.

Paul told King Agrippa that Jesus sent him to the Jewish people and the Gentiles "to open their eyes so that they may turn from darkness to light and from the dominion of Satan to God, that they may receive forgiveness of sins" (Acts 26:18).

Prior to a Billy Graham Crusade in Washington state years ago, my friend Jim Hagensen and I went to a room for counselor training. Everyone was dressed conservatively, but one young man stood out. He was dressed in all white, had a shaved head, and looked like he had either just gotten out of jail, was on drugs, was the milkman, or had been in a hospital for cancer treatment. This man among 3,000 conservatively dressed trainees was suddenly in line right next to me. I tried to share the gospel with him, but he immediately fled as if something had beckoned him to leave. When our training session was over, we went to the foyer where hundreds of people were gathered. The security guards who had been interrogating him told us, "We're absolutely convinced he is demon possessed." I believe this young man was dispatched by the enemy to disrupt the crusade's training orientation.

Pray for Unsaved Family Members

Randy Newman in his book *Bringing the Gospel Home* writes, "Develop a system for prayer for your family. . . . Thank God for his love for each family member." Realize that it may take a long time for a family member to come to Christ.

Dr. Howard Hendricks, President of Dallas Theological Seminary, prayed 42 years for his father, George Hendricks, to come to Christ. In a miraculous way, a chaplain led him to Christ.

Praying for your family is not a guarantee that everyone in your family will come to Christ. We need to rest in the fact that God is completely trustworthy and that He will wipe away every tear from our eyes in heaven.

Pray for Men and Women to Join the Lord's Army of Witnesses for Christ

Jesus said to His disciples, "The harvest is plentiful, but the laborers are few: therefore, pray earnestly to the Lord of the harvest to send out laborers into his harvest" (Matthew 9:37–38 ESV).

Pastor David Jeremiah said, "He is praying that your simple work for Him will bring souls into the kingdom and glory to the Father."

> Author and speaker Lee Strobel said, "Prayer isn't just one more thing we can do. It's the very best we can do."

Pray for the lost. Pray that your family, friends, coworkers, and neighbors will be open to the gospel. Pray for divine opportunities and open doors to share the gospel with your unsaved friends and acquaintances. Write down the names of five people you want to see come to Christ:

- Family member: _____.
- Friend: _____.
- Neighbor: _____.
- Coworker: _____.
- Other: _____.

Write down their needs, concerns, hobbies, and so on. Do they like sports, shopping, or movies? This will help you pray specifically for them and know possible ways to connect with them.

Power Source #3: God's Word

There are two things in this world that are eternal: people and God's Word.

Scripture Memory

My older brother was a new Christian at the age of 16. He would wake me up at 5:00 in the morning and ask me to quiz him on some of the 500 Bible verses he had recently memorized. Seven years later when I became a Christian, my brother was overseas traveling, and I had no one to disciple me. I thought to myself, *what do I do now that I am a Christian?* I decided to engage in scripture memory like my brother had. This was the most important spiritual discipline for my spiritual growth, and it gave me confidence in sharing my faith.

In the Gospel of Luke, Jesus explains the parable of the sower. He said, "Now the parable is this: the seed is the word of God" (Luke 8:11).

Hebrews 4:12 says, "For the word of God is living and active and sharper than any two-edged sword, piercing as far as the division of the soul and spirit, of joints and marrow, and able to judge the thoughts and intentions of the heart."

When evangelist Bill Fay shares his faith, he often asks people to read some key Bible verses out loud.

Then he asks, "What does this say to you?" He says there is something dynamic going on when people read God's Word.

It is because of the work of the gospel through the Holy Spirit and God's Word that a person can come to Christ. Martin Luther said the Bible is like a lion. If people criticize it, you don't defend it; you let it out of its cage. The Holy Spirit will use God's Word to show people their need for Christ (1 Peter 1:23).

Reason from God's Word

Acts 17 says that on three sabbaths Paul "reasoned with them from the Scriptures" (Acts 17:25). He emphasized who Jesus is (the Messiah and God) and what Jesus did for them (suffer and rise from the dead).

Scripture Answers People's Emptiness

People are often searching for meaning in their lives. Augustine said, "Thou hast made us for Thyself, O God, and our hearts are restless till they find their rest in Thee."

Ask someone, "Have you ever read the Bible for yourself?" Some will say yes; most will say no. You can follow up with a question such as this: "Do you know what the Bible's main theme is?" Most will say no, and then you can share the gospel with them and how it addresses their deepest needs—pardon from sin, purpose for living, peace in life, sense of belonging, personal relationship with God, and eternal life. I like the five Ps that only Christ can provide for a person: **Purpose** (for living), **Peace** (with God), **Pardon** (from sin), **Power** (to live the Christian life), and a **Place** in heaven.

In Acts 8, an Ethiopian eunuch was reading a passage from Isaiah 53. Philip, the evangelist, asked him, "Do you understand what you are reading?" (Acts 8:30). Philip explained the gospel to him from God's Word, and the eunuch came to faith in Christ.

God's Word Gives Us Confidence

Memorizing a handful of Bible verses as it relates to the gospel is important. However, if you have difficulty memorizing scripture, you can use a gospel tract. You can also download a Bible app that you can refer to as you share your faith.

Here are some effective ways to memorize scripture:

1. Read the verse aloud several times.
2. Use notes or flash cards to write down key verses.

3. Review those verses daily.

4. Listen audibly as you read them out loud.

5. Pray for the Lord to help you memorize scripture.

6. Go to www.biblememory.com, and download the app.

Paul Nowak, Founder and CEO of IrisReading. com, says "Memorization serves as a workout for the brain. The brain is like a muscle that requires exercise for optimal functioning." Pastor Dudley Rutherford, author of *Compelled*, states, "When you repeat important verses, they will be stored in your long-term memory just like the lyrics of your favorite songs."

Jesus has given us all the resources to share the gospel, including the power of the Holy Spirit, the power of prayer, the power of the Word of God, and the power of His presence. We should focus not on what we can't do but what we can do through Christ. He has given us everything we need to be an effective witness for Christ.

In "Next Steps" at the end of this book is a list of scriptures to memorize.

6
YOUR PERSONAL TESTIMONY

Your personal testimony is one of the greatest tools you have when you share the gospel. People like stories, especially ones that are true. Stories emotionalize information. Jesus often told stories (parables).

No persuasive argument will ever be a substitute for your personal testimony. To be an effective witness, you simply need to tell others what you have seen, heard, and experienced with Jesus (1 John 1:1–3). The famous apologist Josh McDowell said that when he gives his personal testimony and someone asks him how he knows it's true, his answer is this: "I know it's true because I was there."

Recently, I was on a plane from Seattle to Phoenix, and the passenger next to me was a lady from New Zealand. She was in her early 50s and recently divorced. She had just been hired as a tennis instructor at a high-end resort in Scottsdale, Arizona. She had rarely attended church as a child, but she was very interested in talking to me about spiritual matters. I told her that I became a Christian at the age of 19, and she asked me, "How did that happen?" That gave me a wide-open door to share my personal testimony and the gospel with her, and she listened with keen interest. It was a divine appointment.

Examples of Personal Testimonies in Scripture

There are many instances of personal testimonies in Scripture. The woman at the well, for example, believed in the Lord and immediately began telling others about Christ. She went back to her city and said, "Come, see a man who told me all the things that I have done" (John 4:29).

In Mark 5 after Jesus healed the Gerasene demoniac, He told the man, "'Go home to your people and report to them what great things the Lord has done for you and how He had mercy on you.' And he went away and began to proclaim in Decapolis what great things Jesus had done for him" (Mark 5:19–20; Luke 8:39). In the book of John, Jesus healed the man who was born blind, and then the man testified to the skeptical religious leaders. "One thing I do know, that though I was blind, now I see" (John 9:25). This was his personal testimony.

The Apostle Paul shared his personal testimony three times in the book of Acts (Acts 22:1–22; 26:12–18) to segue into the gospel. Paul's testimony serves as a biblical model you can follow in developing your own personal testimony.

Your personal testimony, a subjective experience, is backed up by the objective evidence of the resurrection of Christ and the Word of God. Cults and false religions do not have this truth.

> Greg Laurie wrote, "The point of sharing your story is so you can tell His story . . . we don't want people marveling over our story, but over . . . the price that He paid because of His great love for us."

Your Story

Practical Importance

A well-prepared personal testimony is a true story about how you met the Lord.

The Preparation

Prayerfully ask the Lord for wisdom (James 1:5) as you develop your personal testimony. Outline the main elements of your personal testimony.

The Main Elements in a Personal Testimony

A personal testimony has six main parts:

1. *The opening:* Think of a theme you can use to share your story.

2. *Before you came to Christ:* What your life was like before you met Christ.

3. *How you realized your need for Christ.*

4. *After you became a Christian:* The difference Jesus has made in your life.

5. *The closing*

The Opening

Look at "Some Personal Testimony Themes" at the end of this chapter and select the one that fits your life before coming to faith in Christ.

Before You Came to Christ

What was your life like before you met Christ? For example:

- What was lacking in your life?

- How did you attempt to meet what you were lacking—through wrong friends, marriage and family, work, sports, physical fitness, drugs, sex?

- Don't brag about past sins or struggles. Share just enough to show your need for Christ.

- What common circumstances would a non-Christian relate to—attitudes, what was important to you, how you substituted God for something else?

How You Realized Your Need for Christ

What were the circumstances or details that caused you to consider Christ? Explain the events that led to your conversion. How did God get your attention? Be specific. If you became a Christian as a child, focus more on how Christ has made a difference in your life since you became a Christian at an early age.

After You Became a Christian

In the "Before You Came to Christ" section, you expressed your needs and how you did not find fulfillment. In this section, share how Christ made the difference in your life—how He met your needs. Emphasize the changes in your behavior or character since you received Christ. Share a scripture that was meaningful to you at that time. You may want to paraphrase the verse.

The Closing

End with a statement, a question, or a verse that summarizes your story and relates back to your theme, and that requires a response.

Tips on Sharing Your Story

Outline the main points on a 3" x 5" card. Keep it clear and simple (KISS method) and keep it short (2–3 minutes or 100 words or less).

- Ask for permission to share—"Would it be okay if I shared with you how God changed my life?"

- Be honest, positive, and joyful. Don't lie or embellish. Be truthful.

- Don't criticize a church or denomination.

- Consider practicing in front of a fellow believer for input.

- Be conversational—you are sharing, not preaching, your personal testimony.

- Use ordinary language—avoid religious jargon such as redeemed, saved, born again, justified, sanctified, baptized by the Holy Ghost, and so on.

- Include some humor and human interest.

- Highlight God's presence and power in your life.

- Share before and after stories.

- Compare a life without purpose and direction to a life of deep meaning and purpose.

- Compare self-centeredness to a desire to be more giving and loving.

- Compare the fear of death to peace for the future.

- Compare loneliness to a sense of belonging.

- Compare addiction to something like drugs or pornography to freedom.

- You may have more than one testimony since the Lord is teaching you many things in your life with Him and maturing you in relationship with Him.

- Practice sharing your personal testimony with a friend.

- In your personal testimony, be clear how you received Christ, share the gospel, and invite them to respond.

TESTIMONY WORKSHEET

I. BEFORE I RECEIVED CHRIST—Focus on a need you had or a problem (3–4 sentences).

_____

_____

_____

_____

_____

_____

_____

II. HOW YOU RECEIVED CHRIST OR BECAME A CHRISTIAN (3–4 sentences).

_____

_____

_____

_____

_____

_____

_____

_____

III. AFTER YOU BECAME A CHRISTIAN, WHAT CHANGES OCCURRED OR HOW DID GOD MET YOUR NEED? (3–4 sentences).

_____

_____

_____

_____

_____

_____

_____

Favorite Bible verse:

_____

_____

_____

_____

_____

_____

_____

_____

_____

PERSONAL TESTIMONY THEMES
(pick one main theme)

THEMES/PROBLEMS	HOW CHRIST ANSWERED THIS NEED
	EMOTIONAL THEME
• Worries/Anxiety	Inner Peace
• Grief	Comfort and Joy
• Stress/Burnout	Power and Energy for Life
• Lack of Emotional Support	Faith and Hope to Face Life
• Bitterness/Resentment	Forgiveness and Love
• Anger/Temper	Patience and Love
• Loneliness	God's Contentment and Peace
• Depression	Joy and Freedom
	PSYCHOLOGICAL THEME
• Guilt and Shame	Forgiveness and Freedom
• Low Self-Esteem	Feeling Valued by God
• Pain of Rejection	Sense of Fulfillment
	PURPOSE IN LIFE
• Lack of Purpose/Emptiness	Meaning and Purpose in Life
• Boredom with Life	Sense of Hope and Purpose
• Missing Something in Life	Fulfilled and Adventure with God
	PHYSICAL
• Poor Health	Strength for Each Day

MARRIAGE AND FAMILY

- Marital Problems   Transformed Marriage
- Broken Family   Belonging to (Adopted into) God's Family

FEARS or FEARFUL

- Fear of Dying   Lasting Peace

FINANCIAL/WORK

- Stress, Overworked   Trust in God, Positive Changes

ADDICTIONS

- Sex, Drugs, Habits   Victory and Freedom

MISCELLANEOUS

- Discontent   Confidence and Security
- Self-Centeredness   Serving in a Local Fellowship

7

ATTITUDES AND APPROACHES

Be Humble and Positive

Paul said in Philippians 2:5, "Have this attitude in yourselves which was also in Christ Jesus, who, although He existed in the form of God, did not regard equality with God a thing to be grasped, but emptied Himself, taking the form of a bond servant." Humility and patience with people are important. Remember how you came to Christ. We have the most positive news to share with others.

Communicate the Message of Love.

Our motive for sharing the gospel is love. 2 Corinthians 5:14 (NIV) says, "The love of Christ compels us." Our love for Christ should move us to share the gospel with those who don't know Christ. Some people attribute this quote to St. Francis of Assisi: "Preach the gospel at all times, and if necessary, use words." Some historians state there's no evidence that St. Francis ever said this. No matter who said it, people need to know that God loves them.

> "I am convinced that the greatest act of love we can ever perform for people is to tell them about God's love for them in Christ."—Billy Graham

A student named Steve Walker was sitting outside on the grass one day by himself, waiting for class to start at Cal Poly, Pomona, California. Two students from Cru walked up to him and asked if they could talk to him about something. He asked them what about, and they said, "Jesus." That didn't scare Steve because he had grown up in a very religious family, but he had been taught that Jesus died and suffered on the cross because he (Steve) was a bad person. He believed that God was always mad at him or sad because of his badness. The guilt and shame of his condition was so strong that he never felt there was any chance to please God or any chance that God would love him. These two fellow students shared the Four Spiritual Laws with Steve, and it was the first time he had heard that God loved him. It froze him in his tracks. The students asked Steve if he would like to accept Jesus Christ as his Lord and Savior, to have his sins forgiven and washed away, and have the Lord change him into the person God wanted him to be. Steve's response was a combination of anger and disbelief—anger because no one had ever explained this to him in all his years of religion, and disbelief because he couldn't imagine saying no to such an offer of God's love and forgiveness, as well as God's willingness to change him into a person who was pleasing to Him. Steve prayed to receive God's offer of love and forgiveness. One week later, Steve was walking around campus with the same two students, asking other students if he could talk to them about Jesus. Steve soon got involved in discipleship, and a few months later, he left his engineering major and his college and transferred to a Bible college to study to become a pastor. Eventually, he started an amazing new church that has grown to nearly 5,000 people in Bothell, Washington, and has many amazing ministries that impact people for Christ.

Love in Action

In Matthew, Jesus said we are to love God with all our being. He added, "The second [commandment] is like it, 'You shall love your neighbor as yourself'"

(Matthew 22:39 ESV). The gospel message becomes more receptive when we demonstrate God's love in sacrificial ways. Words coupled with love have a great impact.

We are to be salt and light in the world. "You are the salt of the earth. . . . You are the light of the world. A city set on a hill cannot be hidden. Nor do people light a lamp and put it under a basket, but on a stand, and it gives light to all in the house" (Matthew 5:13–15 ESV).

In 2007, my niece Rebecca Pratt started a ministry called Orphan Relief and Rescue to get children out of human trafficking and domestic abuse in Benin and Liberia, West Africa (a stronghold of voodoo and witchcraft practices). The ministry has rescued hundreds of children who were sold into slavery. Initially, the team decided not to share that they were Christian missionaries because their lives could be at risk. They built friendships, and in time, the parents wanted to know why they were helping their children. The team shared with them the love of Christ, and many parents and children embraced Jesus as their Savior. Orphan Relief and Rescue headquarters is located in Burien, Washington, and can be found online with more details of its ministry.

Lee Strobel writes, "Is there an elderly widow down the block . . . or a junior high student who's looking for someone to shoot baskets with . . . or a single mother who could use a babysitter for her two children . . . or a colleague who's going through a divorce. Someone said, 'People don't care how much you know until they know how much you care.'"

Show an Interest in People's Lives

Recently I returned an item at Home Depot. I asked the cashier in the return section what her name was. She was from India and was a Hindu. She said her name was Kshama. Then she wrote it on a Home Depot business card and gave it to me. She asked, "Do you know what my name means?" I said no. She said it means "forgive me." I then explained to her that Jesus forgave us at the cross of all our sins when He said, "It is finished" (John 19:30 ESV). She said she had never heard the gospel before. I went back to my car and got her a gospel tract on heaven and the Gospel of John, and she thanked me.

When I occasionally strike up a conversation with someone with tattoos, I ask them the significance of the tattoo and then try to somehow connect that to the gospel.

Offer to Pray

I was working out at a local fitness facility and met a Hindu man named Ranga who was 79 years old.

I gave him a booklet my brother wrote called "Why Jesus? Have You Considered Him?" Ranga read the booklet, and then we often talked about what it said. He has lung fibrosis with scarring of the lungs. I asked him if I could pray for him, and he agreed. I touched his shoulder as I prayed for him, and I saw that my prayer touched his heart. Soon after, I gave Ranga the book *More Than a Carpenter* by Josh Mc Dowell. Ranga texted me, "I am reading the book that you gave me; a page every day." Then he noted, "I am the way (John 14:6); Jesus claimed to be the visible expression of God (John 14:9). Jesus is the true manifestation of God himself. . . . Blessed is the one that can surrender with unconditional faith and devotion." The last time I saw Ranga at the fitness facility, he gave me a big hug. I plan on helping him download a Bible app and giving him a copy of the New Testament and a DVD on *The Passion of the Christ* movie. Ranga recently told me he now believes that Jesus is God.

Reaching Gen Zs and Millennials

Gen Zs were born from 1997 through 2012, and Millennials were born between 1981 and 1996. A large percentage of Millennials and almost 50 percent of Gen Zs are religiously unaffiliated (the "nones"), which means they have walked away from the church. Barna research indicates that over 30 percent of Millennials identify as LGBTQ. In *Not Beyond Reach*, Aaron Pierce writes, "We can't wait for people to come to us (church); we have to go to them. . . . We need to learn to share the gospel in ways they will understand." The global youth culture is based on secular humanism, naturalistic evolution, Eastern religious spirituality, and a religion of self.

Jon Sween has a ministry to Gen Zs in the greater Seattle area. He offers this advice in reaching Gen Zs for Christ:

- Pray for an opportunity to connect with Gen Z young adults (Romans 10:1).

- Listen and ask good questions.

- Be a friend and love them.

- Read *Not a Hopeless Case* by Halee Gray Scott on Gen Z.

Look for Divine Appointments

When you pray for divine appointments to share your faith, expect that the Lord will open doors for you to share. The enemy of evangelism is often because our schedules are too full. Make time in your schedule for people. Jesus was often interrupted by people, but He always took time to minister to their needs. Ask the

Lord to show you how you can be more available to the needs of non-believers.

I like Kevin Harney's suggestion in *Organic Outreach* to have a "thirty-second rule" where you say a quick prayer to the Lord such as "Lord, here I am. I'm ready to scatter the seed of your gospel." Then ask yourself, "How might I extend the love of God and the grace of Jesus in this situation?" This is great advice!

Our son Matt and his wife, Amy, joined the ministry of Church Resources Ministries (CRM) in New Orleans and later decided to move to Columbia City, a highly ethnic area of Seattle, Washington. They intentionally chose to live and serve in this area where more than 60 languages were spoken. Matt is now a successful Realtor in the greater Seattle area. Recently he was the recipient of the Good Neighborhood Award for his donations to local ministries such as World Relief, Orphan Relief and Rescue, and other ministries that reach out with the gospel. God has placed us in our work, recreation, and neighborhood to impact those around us with the gospel. Where has God placed you to live, work, and impact others with the gospel?

Be Gracious and Tactful

Share with others as you would have wanted to be shared with before you came to Christ. Colossians 4:6

(ESV) says, "Let your speech always be gracious, seasoned with salt, so that you may know how you ought to answer each person."

I John 4:7 says, "Beloved, let us love one another, for love is from God; and everyone who loves is born of God and knows God. The one who does not love does not know God, for God is love." God's infinite love extends to both the believer and the non-believer.

Warren Wiersbe in his book *Being a Servant of God* says, "Ministry takes place when divine resources meet human needs through loving channels to the glory of God."

Avoid Being Offensive

In 2022, the Seattle Mariners baseball team was celebrating its first playoff game in 21 years. A friend of mine at church and I decided to pass out tracts at the game, but when we arrived at the Mariners' stadium, some men with large banners and loudspeakers were telling the crowd, "The Lord hates all workers of iniquity. America declares its sin like Sodom and Gomorrah!" Most people were repelled by their approach.

God can use wrong motives and methods to reach people, but we need to build a bridge for people, not burn one (Philippians 1:15–18). We need to season the gospel with grace and avoid being offensive. The gospel is good news!

Talk about Jesus

The main thing is to keep the main thing the main thing. During the start of NFL training camp, the legendary and Hall of Fame football coach Vince Lombardi walked into the locker room of the Green Bay Packers, picked up a football, and said, "Gentlemen, this is a football." Greg Laurie's advice is to "keep the main thing the main thing. And the main thing is the gospel faithfully delivered."

The basics of the gospel can be found in 1 Corinthians 2:3 (ESV) where Paul said, "For I decided to know nothing among you except Jesus Christ and him crucified." It's important not to get off on tangents but to focus on Christ, who He is, and what He did for us.

Paul Little in his book *How to Give Away Your Faith* suggests, "In presenting the claims of Christ, it is helpful to use the words of Jesus where possible."

Be Yourself, and Keep It Simple

When I first became a Christian, I memorized a gospel presentation by Dave Hunt, a Christian author and radio commentator. Staff members of Cru were also required to memorize Bill Bright's 20-minute gospel presentation called "God's Plan." These gospel presentations were more for giving a speech than interacting with a person or sharing a simple gospel presentation. You don't need a script to share Christ.

Let God use your natural personality to talk about Jesus. Most people are not gifted salespeople and don't have the gift of gab. Keep it simple and trust the Lord for the results.

Mark Mittelberg writes, "Take a deep breath, say a quick prayer, open your mouth, and let it fly . . . and watch God work."

It's a Team Effort

Look for ways to supplement your witnessing efforts such as inviting your friends to church or a small group to meet other believers; giving them a book; or sharing a blog, a YouTube video, a podcast, or a link to a website. I shared Christ to an Uber driver in Arizona and showed him the Bible app where he can listen audibly to God's Word. He said, "Great! I need to start listening to something other than the news." He thanked me and added the Bible app to his mobile device.

8

ASKING QUESTIONS USING CONVERSATIONS TO SHARE THE GOSPEL

Every day we have conversations about things such as sports, hobbies, health, diets, politics, finances, weather, shopping, family, children, pets—you name it.

I recently was at the airport, and standing next to me was a man in a suit who looked like he worked there. I asked him if he worked at the airport, and he told me he was a limousine driver. I asked him where he was from. He said Uzbekistan, and I asked, "What is the religion of Uzbekistan?" He said about 90 percent are Muslims, and about 10 percent are Russian Orthodox. It turned out that he was an agnostic. I shared the gospel with him and told him,

"Of all the great religious leaders, Jesus is the only who declared He was God and that He would rise from the dead exactly three days after His crucifixion. Mohammed, Buddha, and Confucius are still in the grave, but Jesus's tomb is empty. I've been in Christ's tomb, and it's empty." He then asked, "Dave, did it take you three days to get out?" We laughed, and then I told him about Y-Jesus.com and that it has scholarly articles and videos such as "Did Jesus Rise from the Dead?" "Is Jesus God?" and many other related topics. He asked me if he could take a picture of my phone that showed the website Y-Jesus.com. My prayer is that he will find Jesus someday from this website.

Asking questions shows a genuine interest and helps you understand people's fears, hurts, concerns, and needs in life.

Be a Good Listener

James wrote, "Be quick to hear, slow to speak" (James 1:19). People are more inclined to listen to us and share our beliefs if we listen to them. Lee Strobel said, "Many times the best gift we can give our spiritually seeking friends is our time, a listening ear, and a caring heart."

A recent Barna study states, "People of no faith are clear that they are looking for understanding, empathy, and belonging." Some gospel presentations are like a sermon or a script that allows for little interaction with the person you are sharing Christ with. Let them talk, and consider asking when you do share, "Does this make sense to you?" or "What do you think?"

Expect people to throw out questions, but don't be afraid to ask them questions in return. By asking questions, they may realize that their worldview is not based on rational arguments. Jesus was a master at asking questions. He would often ask them a question in return.

In Randy Newman's book *Questioning Evangelism* is a chapter called "Why Are Questions Better Than Answers?" Newman said, "It's uncanny how often our Lord answered a question with a question." Newman encourages the use of questions more than direct answers. In fact, Jesus used a mix of probing and rhetorical questions when talking to people. When people questioned his authority, Jesus said, "I will ask you a question, and you tell Me; Was the baptism of John from heaven or from men?" (Luke 20:3–4).

Informational Questions

"Who do people say I am?" (Mark 8:27, 29 NIV). "Who do you say I am?" Jesus asked the Samaritan woman at the well. "Will you give me a drink?" (John 4:7 NIV). He then spoke to her about salvation.

Discerning Questions

"And [Jesus] asked them, 'How many loaves do you have?' They said, 'Seven'" (Mark 8:5). We may ask in a given situation, "What do you think?"

Corresponding Questions

"[Jesus] answered them, 'What did Moses command you?'" (Mark 10:3). Jesus said, "What is written in the law? How do you read it?" (Luke 10:26 ESV).

You can ask a person to read a scripture such as Romans 6:23, Ephesians 2:8–9, or Revelation 3:20. Then ask them what they think it means. Bill Fay in *Share Jesus without Fear* asks the person to read the scripture aloud and then asks them, "What does this say or mean to you?"

Conversational Questions

1. Do you have any kind of spiritual belief? At what point are you in your spiritual journey in life? Do you go to church anywhere?

2. When you and I leave this planet, what do you think is on the other side?

3. Do you believe that God exists and that you can know Him personally?

4. Do you consider yourself a good person?

5. What role, if any, has God ever played in your life?

6. Do you ever wonder about life after death?

Questions Relating to Heaven

- On a scale of 1 to 100, how would you rate your certainty of going to heaven?

- What do you think are the general entrance requirements into heaven?

- If you were to die tonight, how sure are you that you would go to heaven?

- If you were to die tonight and God were to ask you, "Why should I let you into heaven?" what would you say to God?

7. Has anyone ever taken the time to explain how a personal relationship with God is possible?

Below are some questions to ask when people go through trials (from Randy Newman's *Questioning Evangelism*):

1. What have you found helpful in handling such difficult things?

2. Do you have the kind of faith that has helped you deal with this?

3. Would you mind if I prayed with you right now?

Bill Fay's book *Share Jesus without Fear* has five main questions he asks people to open up a conversation on spiritual matters.

1. Do you have any kind of spiritual belief? Do you ever think about spiritual things?

2. To you, who is Jesus Christ?

3. Do you think that there is a heaven or a hell? Do you ever ponder about life after death?

4. If you died, where would you go? If you say heaven, why would God let you in?

5. If what you believe is not true, would you want to know?

Emotional Questions

I'm sure you've had people ask you, "How's your day going?" As you get to know people and show them that you care, sometimes they will open up and share what they're going through.

We live in a culture where everyone is tied to their mobile devices and people are lonely and socially starved. The next time you are at a doctor's office, at the airport, or in a restaurant, watch how many people are tied to their cell phones. Listening shows that you care. It allows you to understand more where they're coming from and can be an entry way to the gospel.

Application: Write down 5–7 questions on a 3" x 5" card or on your mobile device so you can review it for a gospel conversation starter.

9

THE PROCESS

Evangelism is usually a process of sowing the seed of the gospel. That takes the pressure off our having to "seal the deal" and keeps us from being discouraged if a person does not receive Christ immediately. It is the Holy Spirit who convicts people of their need for Christ, but it is our responsibility to share the gospel.

There are multiple exposures and many conversations before a person comes to Christ, which could take years. Be encouraged because you may be one of the steppingstones for a person to come to Christ in God's perfect timing.

Some Sow, Others Reap

Already he who reaps is receiving wages and is gathering fruit for life eternal; so that he who sows, and he who reaps may rejoice together. For in this case the saying is true, "One sows, and another reaps." I sent you to reap that for which you have not labored; others have labored, and you have entered into their labor.

—John 4:36–38

Several years ago, I met with a successful businessman named Steve who was in his 30s and not a believer. His wife, Kelly, was a strong believer, and she was faithfully praying for Steve. They both attended a strong, Bible-believing church. For about two years, Steve and I met on a monthly basis for breakfast and reviewed the gospel several times. Eventually, Steve in God's perfect timing received Christ as his personal Savior. It took several seed-planting times for Steve to realize his need for Christ. Steve and Kelly are now faithful servants of Christ at a large church in Washington state.

I was the founding pastor of a new church plant on the east side of Seattle. Fred started attending our church and was open to meet and discuss the gospel with me. We met for about 10 weeks, but Fred was still not ready to receive Christ. Jon Sween, who attended our church, decided to meet with Fred on a regular basis. Finally, after a year and a half, Fred announced to Jon that he had received Christ. You may not be the first person to share Christ with a person, a family member, or a loved one, and you may not be the last one either.

Bill was a robust South African rugby player who was a Jewish atheist. One day he came into my brother's retail store and commented sarcastically, "You guys are Christians, aren't you?" Then he stormed out and remarked, "I am an atheist, and I'm a Jew!" Bill's wife was a godly Christian who had been praying for Bill for many years. I met Bill at his home and began to share Christ with him. His wife told me, "Bill has been wanting someone to share Christ with him." Within a few minutes, Bill broke down sobbing. He was not yet ready to give his life to Christ, but he still had questions and was weighed down by an emotional trauma from his past. I learned that when Bill was a child, his mother used to beat him until his back was bloody. But now, Bill had a loving wife and was surrounded by Christians at work. Not too long after my encounters with Bill, a new Christian shared Christ with Bill and led him to Christ. Immediately after receiving Christ, Bill called to thank me for my involvement in his salvation. Some sow, and some reap—and God gets the glory!

Don't Give Up

When Cru trained me how to share the gospel, we headed to the local beaches in Southern California, took surveys, and then shared the gospel. Over the course of several weeks, one of the lifeguards heard the gospel from various believers 46 times. The lifeguard then said, "Don't ever give up. On the 46th time after hearing the gospel, I received Christ." Evangelist Bill Fay says it takes an average of 7.6 times for a person to hear the gospel before they receive Christ.

A Story of Faithfulness

Salvadore Rivas Gomez was born in 1924, immigrated to the United States, went to Bible school, and became a chaplain. In his later years, Salvadore was unable to drive. Church members often drove him to places like grocery stores where he befriended folks, gave kids candy, and asked questions such as "Do you have a Bible at home?" or "Do you ever pray to God?" He bought boxes of Christian tracts and prayed for the needs of those he spoke to. He distributed food and tracts to people who were looking for work.

He shared the gospel to the poor as they were served meals at the local church, and he provided leftovers and clothing to the homeless camps. He distributed books and tracts at grocery stores, dentists' officers, and barber shops. In his old age, Salvadore could barely walk and had to use a walker, but that did not deter his desire to introduce Jesus to others. At 98 years of age, the Lord called Salvadore home to heaven and probably said, "Salvadore, you've been my servant on earth for a long time. Come and rest for a time. I'll have something for you later. Well done, good and faithful servant. Enter into the joy of thy Master."

The Lord wants us to sow the seed of the gospel. Jesus tells the parable of the four soils (Matthew 13:1–23; Mark 4:1–34; Luke 8:4–18). Only one of the four soils produced fruit. "And the one on whom seed was sown on the good soil, this is the man who hears the word and understands it, who indeed bears fruit and brings forth, some a hundredfold, some sixty, and some thirty" (Matthew 13:23). Witnessing is simply sowing the seed of the gospel and leaving the results to the Lord.

Responses of the heart to the seed of God's Word			
Hard soil	Shallow soil	Infested soil	Good soil
Seed snatched away	Seed grows, withers; no deep roots	Seed crowded out	Seed produces bountiful harvest

"Whoever sows sparingly will also reap sparingly, and whoever sows generously will also reap generously" (2 Corinthians 9:6 NIV). The amount of the harvest is directly proportional to the amount of seed that is scattered.

Sowing and reaping require waiting, just like the farmer who needs to be patient to see the fruit of his labors. My friend Randy Clinesmith, who is a farmer, told me it takes about six months for the harvest. The amount of harvested wheat depends on things such as soil, fertilizer, and the weather. The more seeds he plants, the greater the harvest.

Fertile Soil

Recently I saw on LinkedIn a person I thought I knew from several years ago. I messaged him and said, "Chris, are you the guy I shared Christ with several years ago?" He answered, "Yes, Dave. It was May 13, and he gave me the exact year. At the time, Chris was the newly elected president of his fraternity at UCLA. Our Cru team had made a gospel presentation to the whole fraternity during their weekly gathering on Monday nights. When Chris was a young teen, he had experimented with drugs and alcohol, and he was arrested a few times before he was 18 years old. He was clearly headed in the wrong direction, but the Lord was pulling at the heartstrings of his life. His whole family had come to Christ, and he could see the changes Christ had made in their lives. Chris and I had met for lunch, and after sharing the gospel, I encouraged him to receive Christ. Chris went back to his fraternity, and in the privacy of his room, he reviewed the gospel and, on his knees, prayed, "Lord Jesus, I need You. Thank You for dying on the cross for my sins. I open the door of my life and receive You as my Savior and Lord. Thank You for forgiving my sins and giving me eternal life. Take control of the throne of my life. Make me the kind of person You want me to be."

When Chris prayed that prayer to receive Christ and got off his knees, he said he felt like he had been hiking all day with a heavy backpack and then it had been taken off his back. He knew that Christ had come into his life. Chris began leading some of his fraternity buddies and others at UCLA to Christ. He got involved with Cru and taught Bible studies. For the last several years, he and his wife have been faithfully involved in serving the Lord in their local church and supporting various ministries. Jesus said in John 6:44, "No one can come to me unless the Father who sent me draws them." God is the supreme evangelist. Ultimately, it's the Lord who draws people to Himself, but He wants to use us in the process to sow the seed of the gospel. One of my favorite visual illustrations is called the Engel

Scale. There are many examples of the Engel Scale on the web.

PROCESS EVANGELISM				
Many more post-conversion steps are needed for spiritual maturity				
				A NEW DISCIPLE IS BORN
Our Role				Seeker's Condition
Be a Friend and Be Available	Demonstrate God's Love and Power	Explain Practically	Persuade	1 Asking forgiveness of sin and having faith in God
				2 Challenge and decision to act
				3 Awareness of his or her need for God
				4 Positive attitude toward Christianity
				5 Grasps the cost to be a Christian
				6 Awareness of the basic facts of Christianity
				7 Interest in Christianity
				8 Initial awareness of Christianity
				9 No effective knowledge of Christianity
				10 Awareness of spirituality
				11 No belief or interest in spirituality

After sharing the gospel with a person, I often ask myself where that person is after they heard the gospel. They may have "no belief or interest in spirituality," but after sharing the gospel with them, they may have moved, for example, to #4 on the Engel Scale where they have a positive attitude toward the gospel and Christ. At times, I have shown a person the Engel Scale after sharing the gospel with them and then asked where they are on the scale. Then I say, "What do you think it would take for you to receive Christ?" Rarely does a person suddenly move from "no belief or interest in spirituality" to an immediate decision to ask the Lord to be Lord of their life. Usually there are many steps before they receive Christ.

In Mark 12:28, a scribe who was an expert in the Mosaic Law asked Jesus, "What commandment is the foremost of all?" Jesus masterfully answered the question. As He dialogued with the scribe, He said, "You are not far from the kingdom of God" (Mark 12:34). Jesus peered into the scribe's heart and saw that he was moving closer to surrendering his life to Jesus, the Messiah.

Once I had a conversation with a young man who said he was an atheist. I asked him, "If you could know God personally, would you be interested?" He responded by saying yes. I shared the gospel with him, and he was almost ready to receive Christ. He had moved from a stated atheist to grasping an understanding of how to become a Christian. If possible, keep a relationship open with people you talk to.

Christ Fills the Void in People's Lives

Years ago, my wife and I lived in Southern California after we had moved from the Great Northwest in Portland, Oregon. My new assignment with Cru was to share Christ on the campuses of UCLA and

Moorpark College. We purchased our first home in the town of Moorpark and moved in with our two young children. The house was a few blocks from the college. One of the students who received Christ at Moorpark was a young man named John Ruttkay. Over the years, we lost contact with one another, but recently I tried to locate him. I didn't know whether John was even still alive or if he still lived in California. I did a search for John on the White Pages and finally found him. I called his phone number and left a voicemail that explained the purpose of my call. A person called me back and excitedly said, "Dave, it's John Ruttkay!" We both rejoiced greatly together. Needless to say, it made my day. John then shared his full, amazing testimony with me.

In 1974, I was setting out on my grand adventure from the Washington, DC, area to hitchhike across the nation to California to play football at a junior college in a little town called Moorpark. There were three of us from the DC area that were going to try to make that team. It was an interesting time in our culture. We were coming into the tail end of the hippie movement but still holding strongly to the zeitgeist of that time, which was sex, drugs, and rock 'n' roll.

It was a revolutionary time with many things happening geopolitically. It was pushing many people my age—late teens, early twenties—to start asking the bigger questions of why we are here and what is our purpose. I certainly was one asking those very questions and as a result started on my spiritual quest. . . . By the time I reached 17, I was experimenting with drugs. I was having some spiritual experiences through drugs and began to realize there was a whole supernatural realm that left me hungry to pursue alternatives from my past experience.

I started exploring transcendental meditation first but had no appetite for just sitting around and going inward. A friend of mine came to me. He was also on that quest and took me to Buddhist meetings. That was more my style. It was more bent to my moral and philosophical mindset at the time. I believed everyone was looking for Nirvana and thought they could do it by their own means. At 19, I was no different. It wasn't long before I got my whole family and friends involved in Buddhism. I became a bona fide evangelist for Buddha.

In 1974, I started my trek to California. I was a devout Buddhist with a backpack and a sleeping bag, and I was ready to conquer the world and hopefully make the football team. On my way to California, by the time I hit Nebraska there was a whole lot of talk about Jesus by people picking me up. I was aware that there were people called Jesus Freaks on the West Coast but never gave it a second thought. By the time I got to Salt Lake City, I was cleaning up in a bus station and ran into a hippie kind of a guy, and I was like he was. He asked me if we could hitchhike to San Francisco together. He was hesitant at first but forthrightly shared, "I am a believer in Jesus Christ and just want you to know I'm going to tell you about Him." I said, "Awesome! I'm a Buddhist, and I will tell you about him." Little did I know that I was going to a knife fight and the other guy's got a gun. We had engaging conversations, and I stayed with his family the entire week. They invited me to a midweek service in their neighborhood. It was the time of the Jesus Movement, so there was literally a great awakening taking place that would soon sweep the entire nation. Everyone at the meeting that night was my age or a little older. The preacher came out, and he was a hippie and started preaching about Jesus and what it takes to know Him. I was intrigued for sure but still had questions.

The next day, I left for Southern California with a lot of questions, enough so I decided to hitchhike to the Buddhist monastery in Santa Monica. I asked them to explain to me about born again Christians because I had never heard the term. Their only admonition was to stay away from them; they were very persuasive. I decided my spiritual pursuits would have to take a back seat because I had a football team to make. I made the team, and one of the guys from the East Coast was my roommate. The coaches got us a house that we shared with a couple of the basketball players. It was a lot of fun. . . . After the football season was over, that haunting spiritual void started to return. Pascal, the French philosopher, said,

"There is a God shaped vacuum in the heart of every man which cannot be filled by any created thing, but only by God, the Creator, made known through Jesus."

That's what was happening to me—the partying, the girls, all the accoutrements that go along with an athlete playing college football were becoming white noise to the cry in my heart.

We finished spring ball. I was the starting QB, was excited for the next football season, but couldn't shake that gnawing void in my heart. Finally, one day while walking up to the campus, I let out a cry to God. "Lord, I don't know You, so You need to tell me who You are." I went to the center of campus to hang out with my boys, and I noticed a guy, somewhat conservative, looking ready to violate my space. He came over and introduced himself as Dave Chapman. He asked me a few questions that were about me personally, like what I was studying and things that would open up to a broader conversation. Little did I know that broader conversation would lead into the reality of getting born again. Dave didn't know that 45 minutes prior to that conversation, I was having a conversation with the God of the universe to tell me who He was. After Dave and I prayed a simple prayer, I knew that I knew Jesus saved me. He was pursuing me all along. It all made complete sense with that encounter that day. On a tract, Dave made sure to share the three Fs—Faith (our trust in the trustworthiness of God Himself and His Word), Fact (God and His Word), Feeling (the result of our faith and obedience).

One of the providential things is that Dave lived just three houses down from my house. For the next month, I couldn't get enough of the Scriptures. I had so many questions. Thank God for Dave and his sweet wife for just embracing me like they did. I told the coaches I was not going to be there for summer ball because I got saved and was on a mission—the mission to get my family saved and get them out of Buddhism. It was with prayer and fasting that they all came out and got saved and filled with the Holy Spirit. All my friends got saved, and when I came back for football, I led many teammates to Jesus. There was already a tremendous momentum because of the Jesus Movement, so it made our community grow substantially. I believe that having someone alongside me early on my journey, discipling me, was my key to spiritual growth. After all, the Lord said to go and make disciples, not converts. After my second year,

I transferred schools because football was no longer my priority, and following Christ became my all-consuming passion. Again, I want to reiterate that there was a major move of God happening at the time, and I was at the center of it in Southern California, so the spiritual prevailing winds were in my favor, and there were thousands coming to Jesus. There was a group of us that fall semester who started a Christian club on campus, and within three months, we had outgrown the classroom and filled the quad to share the love of Jesus. We built a strong community from that group and saw many move on into ministry, including myself.

I enrolled in Melodyland Theological School and ended up getting a degree in Religious Studies from Vanguard University. For the last 43 years, I have traveled all over the world to preach the gospel of the Kingdom (Matthew 24:14). I have established drug rehab centers that have impacted thousands of people's lives. I am currently establishing house churches all over Southern California, trying to get back to basic, foundational teachings to get the ekklesia equipped for the coming storm. The kids I am discipling said they thought it was important that my voice get out to the broader Body of Christ. They shared for their generation that it has to come from a digital platform on the Internet. They called it the New Romans Road. The last year and a half, I have explored this venue to communicate to the Body of Christ and the world what the Holy Spirit is saying and doing. There have been hundreds of thousands of views and an overwhelming response from the Body of Christ. I believe we are on the cusp of the greatest outpouring ever seen, and God has called us all to this time. There is a great harvest out there, and the King of Glory is beckoning us to bring in that harvest.

At least four great principles come out of John's story and testimony:

1. We will greatly rejoice someday.

John and I were filled with joy when we reconnected after several years of being disconnected. Jesus said, "I tell you that in the same way there will be more rejoicing in heaven over one sinner who repents than over ninety-nine righteous persons who do not need to repent" (Luke 15:7 NIV). Think of the joy we will have when we get to heaven and see those we shared Christ with on earth who are now in heaven with us. Let's keep sharing the greatest news ever!

2. More seeds planted equals a greater harvest.

Evangelism takes patience. Most people don't come to Christ the first time they hear the gospel. There may be many seeds planted in a person's heart before they receive Christ. We may be the blessed ones who see them come to Christ. In John's case, several people had planted seeds in his life before he received Christ. Sharing Christ is an act of faith and obedience. Let's remember Galatians 6:9: "Let us not lose heart in doing good, for in due time we will reap if we do not grow weary."

3. People are searching for meaning and purpose in life.

Many people are trying to fill the void in their life with things that end up causing them to feel even more empty and unhappy. Jesus is the only One who can fill that God-shaped vacuum in our hearts.

John was the starting quarterback who experimented with drugs, sex, transcendental meditation, and Buddhism, but none of those things filled the void in his life. Only the resurrected living Christ could and did fill that void. Since coming to Christ, John has never looked back. He has had a massive impact on the world. I was privileged to be in the right place at the right time after John uttered his plea to God.

4. Some bear much fruit.

Jesus said in Matthew 13:8, referring to good soil, "And others fell on the good soil and yielded a crop, some a hundredfold, some sixty, and some thirty." John said in his testimony that there is a great harvest out there, and the King of Glory is beckoning us to bring in that harvest. I'm so glad I reconnected with my friend and brother in Christ, John Ruttkay. What a joy unspeakable and full of glory!

Are you a seed planter? Are you sharing the gospel or your personal testimony? Are you reaching out to others in love? Are you speaking to their needs and interests? Are you a good listener? Are you authentic? Are you showing an interest in people by having coffee or lunch with a coworker or neighbor? Are you doing kind gestures of love such as giving them a book, inviting them to church, praying for them, having fun together, or writing them a thank you note? There are myriads of ways to plant seeds in people's hearts. When people see the light of the gospel in you, they will notice something different and perhaps open their hearts to the gospel message.

Here are some ways we can sow the seed in people's hearts, so they are better prepared to receive the gospel.

- Share a scripture verse with them.
- Offer to pray for them about a need.
- Invite them to church or a special event at your church.
- Invite them to join you in a small group in your home.

- Email them an article or video from a website or send them a podcast about knowing Christ.

- Walk through a gospel presentation with them.

- Visit them in the hospital and pray with them.

- Take them a meal when there is a crisis of some sort.

- Give them a book on apologetics such as *More Than a Carpenter* by Josh McDowell or *The Case for Faith* by Lee Strobel.

10

ARTICULATING THE GOSPEL

What's Your Style?

In the book *Becoming a Contagious Christian* by Mark Mittelberg and Lee Strobel are six evangelistic styles: (1) direct (Peter in Acts 2); (2) intellectual or apologetical (Paul in Acts 17); (3) testimonial (blind man in John 9); (4) interpersonal or friendship (Luke 5:27–29); (5) invitational (Andrew told Peter, "We have found the Messiah"); and (6) service- or life-based.

God wants to use your unique personality to share the gospel. My wife's spiritual gifts are different than mine. She is very caring and relational. She demonstrates the love of Christ by her warm, sweet heart and desire to help people. She is not as vocal as I am in sharing the gospel but shares God's love to people when the occasion arises.

Regardless of what style you relate to the most, everyone needs to be able to articulate the gospel. If you knew someone who was dying of cancer in the hospital and there was no pastor around to call upon, what would you say to that person who was soon facing eternity? You need to know the gospel message and share it by using your own style and personality.

James Kennedy, founder of the Evangelism Explosion ministry, once said, "I like my way of doing evangelism better than your way of not doing it."

Many Methods

We learn from Jesus that He used a variety of methods with different people to share the gospel. Paul said in 1 Corinthians 9:22 (ESV), "I have become all things to all people, that by all means I might save some."

Try to adapt the gospel message to the person you are sharing with because everyone is different. In fishing for fish, a good fisherman uses a variety of bait such as worms, lures, salmon eggs, and more because some fish may want worms instead of eggs. The goal is to catch fish. Some people use Ray Comfort's method of evangelism; others use the Bridge, Evangelism Explosion, the Internet, or social media to share Christ. Be willing to learn different methods to share your faith.

Nicodemus and the Woman at the Well

Jesus spoke differently to the woman at the well (an immoral Samaritan woman) than He did to Nicodemus, a ruler of the Jews. In John 4:7 (ESV), Jesus said to her, "Give me a drink?" Jesus transitioned from the known (physical water) to the unknown (living water). She had been seeking fulfillment by going from husband to husband. Jesus did not condemn her. He began where she was and dialoged with her. With Nicodemus, Jesus referenced His impending death on the cross using scriptures from Numbers 21:4–9. In John 19, we see Nicodemus assisting in the burial of Christ.

Reaching Intellectuals

When Paul spoke to the intellectuals of his time, he began with common ground. In Acts 17:16–31, he spoke to the Athenians by stating that they were very religious, and then he mentioned their inscription, "To an unknown God." Paul moved from general revelation to special revelation.

GOSPEL RESOURCES

Tracts

Evangelist George Whitfield and the great Hudson Taylor were both saved through gospel tracts. On one recent occasion, a young lady named Ashlee who had been on drugs and was about to give up on herself read a gospel tract that was left at the door of her apartment by Christians from India at my local church. Ashlee committed her life to Christ and was soon baptized at my church. She said, "I can't live without Jesus now."

If you're not good at memorizing a gospel outline, don't use that as an excuse not to share. You can easily access gospel tracts online that will walk a person through the gospel. If you have a tract, ask this of the person you are conversing with: "If you have a few minutes, I'd love to see what you think about the main points of this booklet." Invite them to coffee or lunch and highlight the main points. Pastor and evangelist Greg Laurie said his first experience in sharing his faith was when he went to the beach and simply read a tract to a lady sitting on the sand. To his amazement, she received Christ.

Some Popular Tracts

Some very popular tracts are "The Four Spiritual Laws" and "Would You Like to Know God Personally?" Over two billion "Four Spiritual Laws" tracts have been distributed worldwide since they were first printed in the 1950s. I had the privilege of sharing this tract with hundreds of college students each year while I was on staff with Cru. If you are not familiar with the "Four Spiritual Laws," here's a brief outline. It begins with this statement: "Just as there are physical laws that govern the physical universe, so are there spiritual laws that govern your relationship with God."

Following that are four main points:

Law 1: God loves you and offers a wonderful plan for your life.

Law 2: Man is sinful and separated from God. Therefore, he cannot know and experience God's love and plan for his life.

Law 3: Jesus Christ Is God's only provision for man's sin. Through Him you can know and experience God's love and plan for your life.

Law 4: We must individually receive Jesus Christ as Savior and Lord; then we can know and experience God's love and plan for our lives.

Cru's tract. "Would You Like to Know God Personally?" can be downloaded from your mobile device at sites such as GodTools (http://godtoolsapp.com).

Other good tracts include "Steps to Peace with God" by the Billy Graham Evangelistic Association; "The Bridge Illustration" by the Navigators; and "Do You Know?" by Evangelism Explosion International.

The Romans Road

Some people share Christ using scriptures from the book of Romans (Romans 3:23; 5:8; 6:23; 8:1; 10:9). You can download Romans Road from the app store on your mobile device.

Share Jesus without Fear by William Fay and Ralph Hodge

This book shares a natural, nonthreatening way to share the gospel. The authors use five simple questions followed by seven Bible verses for a person to read aloud (Romans 3:23; 6:23; John 3:3; 14:6; Romans 10:9–11; 2 Corinthians 5:15; Revelation 3:20). Go to www.sharejesuswithoutfear.com to learn more.

Evangelism Explosion International

When I was pastor of evangelism at a large church, I taught the Evangelism Explosion method to many believers. It has five main points relating to the gospel.

GRACE—Salvation is a free gift that cannot be earned (Romans 6:23).

MAN is a sinner (Romans 3:10, 23); he cannot save himself (Isaiah 64:6).

GOD is love (1 John 4:8) but is also holy (Habakkuk. 1:13) and must punish sin.

CHRIST—Who He is: God (John 1:1–3, 14); what He did: He is our substitute (2 Corinthians 5:21).

FAITH—Temporal faith versus saving faith (John 1:12; Romans 10:9–10, 13). www.evangelismexplosion.org *features great resources for teachers and students.*

The Way of the Master

The Way of the Master by Ray Comfort uses the Mosaic Law to show how a person has broken God's laws and show them their sin and need for repentance. Ask the person you are witnessing to, "If God were to judge you by the standard of the ten commandments, do you think you would be found innocent or guilty, and would you be going to heaven or hell?" This is followed up by a presentation of the gospel. Go to www.wayofthemaster.com to learn more.

One-Verse Evangelism

One-Verse Evangelism is a simple, interactive way to share Christ's love conversationally and visually. It is very easy to learn. It is based on Romans 6:23 (NKJV) "For the wages of sin is death, but the free gift of God is eternal life in Christ Jesus our Lord." You can find this at www.navigators.org/resource/one-versevangelism.

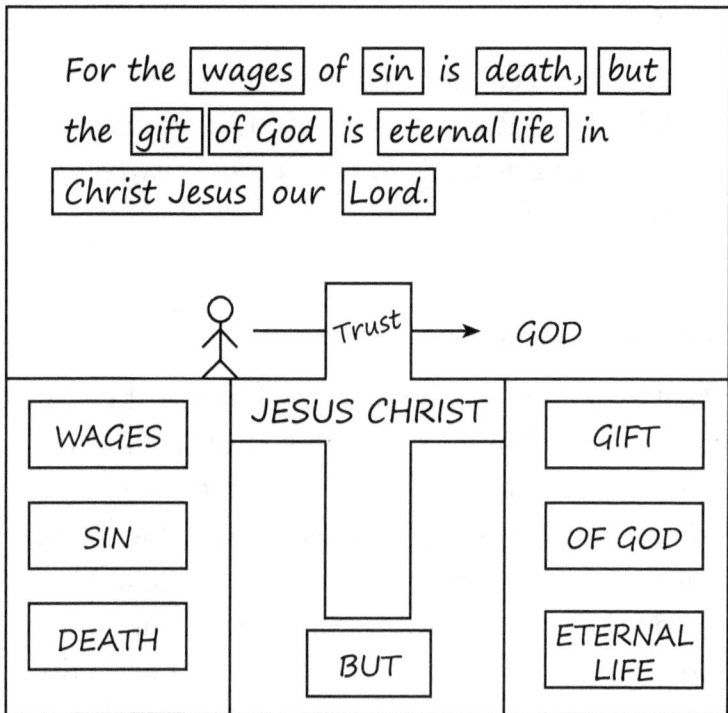

Three Circles Gospel Presentation

This is a simple tool that helps Christians share the gospel using three simple circles that represent (1) God's design, (2) our brokenness, and (3) the gospel. At the end of a gospel presentation, the Christian asks, "Is there anything that would prevent you from repenting and believing the gospel today?" You can learn more about this unique gospel presentation by going to www.namb.net/evangelism/3circles/.

The book *Turning Everyday Conversations into Gospel Conversations* by Jimmy Scroggins and Steve Wright explains a three-circle method and how they relentlessly train believers to share the gospel.

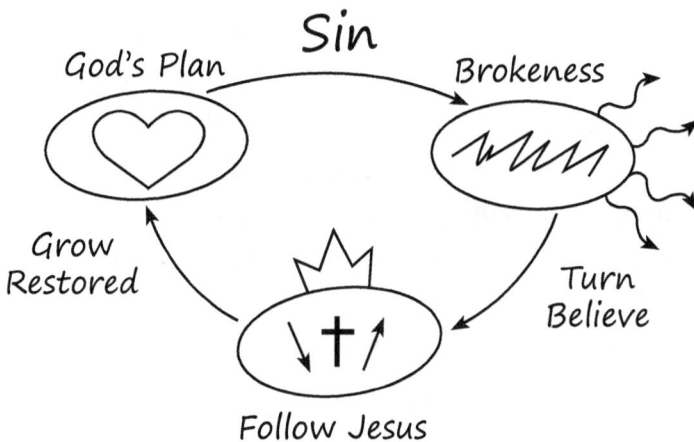

Reaching Jewish People for Christ

The Apostle Paul wrote that the gospel is to go to "the Jew first" (Romans 1:16 ESV). God has not done away with His people, Israel. Romans 11 speaks of a future remnant of Jewish people who will turn to Jesus as their Messiah. The book of Revelation reveals that God is going to commission 144,000 Jewish evangelists to preach the gospel to the entire world during the final few years of human history. Author Joel Rosenberg says there are currently about a million Jews worldwide who believe in Jesus as their Messiah.

I recently shared Christ at a 24-Hour Fitness gym to a young Jewish man in his early 20s named Roy. He knew very little about the Bible. I sent him an article called "Did Jesus Rise from the Dead?" and encouraged him to read the Gospel of Matthew. Whenever I talk to a person who is Jewish, I tell them I love the Jewish people. I quote Genesis 12:2–3 where God told Abraham, "I will make you into a great nation, and I will bless you; I will make your name great, and you will be a blessing. I will bless those who bless you, and whoever curses you I will curse; and all peoples on earth will be blessed through you."

I tell them that I'm praying for their country and for the peace of Jerusalem. This usually gives me an opportunity to share the gospel with them.

Here are a few of the many great ministries to the Jewish people:

- Chosen People Ministries seeks to reach Jewish people for Christ. Their top-selling book is *Isaiah 53 Explained* by Mitch Glaser (www.ChosenPeople.com).

- Jewish Voice's aim is to share the gospel of Yeshua (Jesus) to the Jew first and also to Gentiles (www.jewishvoice.org).

- One for Israel uses cutting-edge media evangelism in Hebrew, Arabic, and English to reach their people for Christ (www.one-forisrael.org).

- The Joshua Fund (www.joshuafund.com) and Jews for Jesus (www.jewsforjesus.org) are ministries that proclaim the gospel of Messiah to the Jewish people.

- Bridgesforpeace.com is a ministry where Christians support Israel and build relationships between Christians and Jews in Israel and around the world.

Pray that the eyes of the Jewish people will be opened to the gospel and that there will be a revival among the Jews to come to Christ. Give Jews a copy

of the New Testament and share your personal testimony—how Jesus changed your life and why you
believe that Jesus is the promised Messiah.

Reaching Muslims for Christ

Many Muslims have a zeal for God, but the gospel,
who Jesus really is, and the concept of grace are foreign
to them. Muslims respect Jesus as a great prophet, and
the Quran has verses on Jesus as a prophet, but they do
not know that Jesus claimed to be God—the "I AM"
statements Jesus made in John 14:6, John 10:30, and
John 8:58 that demonstrate that He is God.

In *The Camel: How Muslims Are Coming to Faith
in Christ*, author Kevin Greeson shares how thousands of Muslims in the Middle East are coming to
Christ. The book shows specific verses in the Quran
that speak positively of Jesus and the Bible to help
Muslims read and understand the gospel.

Many Muslims today are coming to Christ through
dreams. While our son Matt was serving the Lord
with Church Resources Ministries (CRM), he met
an Iranian named Ali who was Muslim. Matt began
praying that Ali would have a dream about Jesus. A
few months later, Matt and Ali watched the movie *The
Passion of the Christ*. That night Ali had a dream about
Jesus and told Matt, "You're not going to believe what
happened to me last night. Last night, Jesus appeared

to me in my dreams, and He showed me the wounds in His hands and feet. I felt His peace, and I knew the story was true. I believe 100 percent that Jesus died and rose again for my sins." Yes, many Muslims are coming to Christ through dreams. YouTube and Instagram portray many testimonies of Muslims coming to Christ. Go to www.ifoundthetruth.com, which is a great website on how Muslims all over the world are encountering Jesus. You can watch their stories now on YouTube.

Tips on Sharing with Hindus and Buddhists

With Hindus:
There are one billion Hindus in the world. In the book, Disciple Making Among Hindus by Timothy Shultz, he provides the following tips to reach Hindus for Christ.

- Hindus view truth through the lens of experience and relationships are very important, especially family and friends. Build authentic and sustainable relationships with Hindus over time. Look for a "person of peace who will invite you into their network of relationships such as family and friends." George David, a pioneer missionary in North India said: "We need to learn the art of narrating the stories of Jesus in a simple . . . manner."

Hindus believe that all people are trapped in a cycle of reincarnation and karma, and the way to break this cycle is in one of three ways: (1) to purify one's soul, they must obey all the laws and obligations of the Hindu scriptures called Vedas; (2) they teach the total rejection and denial of your individual self; (3) they teach that you must commit yourself totally to the worship of a particular god or goddess, and that deity will release them from reincarnation or the karma cycle. Share with a Hindu that in Christ's resurrection, Jesus broke the power of karma and rebirth, or sin and death, because He returned to life in the same body in which He died.

I once asked a Hindu if he did something bad, what would he have to do to make up for the bad deed. He replied, "I would need to do 50 good deeds to make up for the one bad deed." Here's some helpful advice for sharing Christ with a Hindu:

1. Ask and listen to what they believe about God, sin, salvation. You could ask the following:

   • What do you like about Hinduism? What is the most difficult thing for you to accept or practice in Hinduism?

- What do you think happens after you die?

- Who do you think Jesus is? Have you ever read what the Bible says about Jesus?

2. Explain what it means to be born again because a Hindu believes in reincarnation. Jesus taught a totally different definition to Nicodemus in John 3. Hebrews 9:27 says, "It is appointed for men to die once and after this comes judgment."

3. Share Jesus's forgiveness. Bakht Singh, an Indian evangelist who converted from Hinduism to Christ, said, "I have never yet failed to get a hearing [with a Hindu] if I talk to them about forgiveness of sins and peace and rest in your heart." Matthew 11:28 (ESV) says, "Come to me, all who labor and are heavy laden, and I will give you rest."

4. Focus on a personal relationship with God. The parable of the prodigal son in Luke 15:11–32 illustrates how the son rebelled against his father, but the father longed to be reunited with his son. Sin disrupts our relationship with God, but when we confess our sin and guilt, we can receive forgiveness because Jesus paid the full price for our sins.

If we ask the Lord for forgiveness, He will completely forgive us and give us eternal life with Him.

5. All the avatars or incarnations of Vishnu are mythical in nature, but history shows that Jesus lived, was crucified, and rose from the dead. Jesus claimed to be "the resurrection and the life" (John 11:25).

6. Gandhi said, "I shall say to the Hindus that your lives are incomplete unless you reverently study the teachings of Jesus" (Hingorani, 23). Encourage your Hindu friend to read the Gospel of John and share your personal testimony with them.

Rob Adams in his seminar on reaching Hindus recommends sharing stories in the Gospels about Jesus and suggests showing your Hindu friends the Jesus Film, The Chosen series, and also Share the Story (www.biblicalstorying.com) to reach Hindus with the gospel.

When sharing with a Buddhist, keep in mind that their worldview is totally different. A Buddhist does not believe in a personal God. Instead of using terms such as born again, focus on the idea of freedom from guilt, forgiveness, and the gift of eternal life. Talk about the person of Christ and His resurrection from the dead. Share your personal testimony. Offer to give them a Gospel of John to read. There are several online resources for how to share Christ with a Buddhist. Christiananswers.net is an excellent website on how to witness to a Buddhist.

Wrap Up

As you share the gospel, you can ask the person a few questions to find out where they are on their spiritual journey. You might say, "Does this make sense to you?" If they are ready to receive Christ, it's helpful to review with them what a commitment to Christ means. Do they understand that they have sinned and want forgiveness for their sins? Do they believe that Jesus is God and rose from the dead? Do they now want to put their faith in the Lord as their Savior and Lord? If they would like to receive Christ into their life, ask them to pray audibly with you, **or** they can pray in their own words. It's important to follow up with them and get them connected to a local church.

If they are not ready, you can ask, "Why do you feel you are not ready to receive Christ?" They may say, "I don't know enough." They may still not understand the gospel. When I was 12 years old, a Presbyterian pastor visited our house and shared the gospel with my twin sister and me. I prayed the prayer, but I didn't understand what he was sharing. It wasn't until seven years later that I actually committed my life to Christ.

When I think a person understands the gospel, I review the prayer with them and say something like this: "When you invite the Lord into your life, He promised to come to indwell you, to forgive you of your sins, and to give you eternal life as a free gift. He will be in you the rest of your life." Review with them the promises of God such as John 1:12, Revelation 3:20, and John 3:16. Follow-up is important.

1. Invite them to your church and be willing to disciple them.

2. Introduce them to other believers in Christ.

3. Be a friend, and model what a Christian looks like.

4. Give them a *New Believers Bible*.

5. Encourage them to get baptized out of obedience to Christ.

6. Encourage them to get into a home Bible study at your church.

11

HOW CHRISTIANS AND CHURCHES REACH OUT

There are countless ways that Christians and churches can reach out with the gospel. People all over the world are sharing Christ one on one; in large gatherings; and through the media, radio, TV, Bible translations, podcasts, YouTube, TikTok, and the Internet. There is one gospel but many ways to share it.

Equipping People for Evangelism

It is very important that believers are trained to share their faith. Ephesians 4:11–12 says that we're to equip the saints, and that includes evangelism. Most churches are not evangelistic because their members are not equipped to share their faith.

Passing the Baton

While I was on staff with Cru, I met Jim and Tori Wright who were sophomores at Portland State University. At 19 years of age, Jim had just committed his life to Christ. Whenever I saw Jim on campus, I said to him, "Let's go witnessing." And then we would go share the gospel with students on campus. Jim always did great in sharing the gospel, and he quickly caught the bug for full-time ministry. The trajectory of his life had dramatically changed, which began a lifelong adventure that included sharing the gospel as a way of life. Jim and Tori graduated from seminary, and since then Jim has been in five full-time ministries, faithfully serving the Lord for more than 40 years. Now retired, Jim teaches evangelism at his church and is fully engaged in serving the Lord on mission trips to places such as the Zimbabwe, South Sudan, Namibia, Liberia, Chad, and France to equip pastors in biblical theology and evangelism. Jim has faithfully and zealously carried the torch of the gospel, passing the baton on to others. Jim and Tori have clearly modeled 2 Timothy 2:2, which says, "The things which you have heard from me in the presence of many witnesses, entrust to faithful men who will be able to teach others also."

The Uber Pastor

Jayson Turner is a close friend of our family who helped mentor our son Matt into full-time ministry. He is an associate pastor gifted in preaching who also drives for Uber. For the last eight years and with around 10,000 rides, he has shared Christ countless times. Instead of closing the deal, most of his conversations are pre-evangelistic in nature. Jayson commented, "Harvesting is wonderful, but the harvest never arrives if the gardeners (seed planters) are not present the rest of the year." Jayson often gives his riders a small New Testament Bible along with either Tim Keller's book *The Reason for God* or *Mere Christianity* by C. S. Lewis and a gospel tract. Around the holidays, he hands out *Hidden Christmas* by Tim Keller. Jayson also gives people his business card so they can get in touch with him for a follow-up phone call or a time for coffee. Here's a recent post from Jayson:

> Often, I am surprised at how open people are to share the details of their lives with me. A young woman entered my car recently and proceeded to share much from the therapy appointment I picked her up from. Somehow our conversation moved to one's view of God in relation to all the difficulties people experience in life. I got the chance to tell her about how God entered into all this difficulty in the

person of Jesus—the One who had nowhere to lay his head (Luke 9:58); Jesus, the One who came in the form of a servant (Phillipians2:7); Jesus, the One who came to ultimately die for the rebels, rejects, and outcasts to offer all of us new life (Romans 5:8).

After sharing this news about Jesus, my passenger responded, "That's amazing that Jesus would do that for me." Her statement came out in the form of a whisper as though I had just told her an important secret that she was now restating back to me. I was caught off guard by her response. In fact, I was convicted. This young woman had responded to the good news as though it was the best news she had heard in a long while. God's grace had surprised her heart, and I could hear the wonder and delight in her hushed voice. I was convicted because I forgot. I share the gospel often in my Uber conversations, and even then, I forget. I forget that the gospel is indeed the best news ever. It is news of the greatest joy. It is for all people of all time. And it is a remarkable thing to learn that there is a God in heaven who didn't skirt the stench of this planet but rather gave everything to rescue us. May we walk in that wonder this advent month. And perhaps as we meditate on the scandal of God taking the form of a man, we too will worship Him afresh in a massive joy. I am thankful for Jesus. Joy!

Jayson concluded his post with Luke 2:10 (ESV). "And the angel said to them, 'Fear not, for behold, I bring you good news of great joy that will be for all the people.'"

To learn more of the creative ways that Jayson shares the gospel, I encourage you to go to either www.uberpastor.com or Instagram@uberpastor. You'll see several of Jayson's posts that are very helpful and insightful in sharing the gospel.

Gospel Tracts are Effective

A good friend of mine, Tom Harmer, staples a $5 bill to a Gospel tract where the people can see the $5. He often will go to Home Depot early in the morning where there is a crowd of five to ten people standing at the entry hoping to get a day job from customers. Tom pulls his car up and they all gather around his driver's window. He smiles and holds up a handful of tracts with the $5 bill poking out and he says, "Hi, guys, I don't have any work for you today, but I do have $5 for each of you and special instructions in this tract which are far more valuable than $5 bucks. If you read and follow these instructions, then you will gain eternal life and have all your sins paid for by

Jesus!" They all reach out and take a tract and Tom shares the gospel and finishes by saying, "You can count on God's promises! Repent + Believe & Receive = Heaven." Tom tells me: By doing this, "I'm storing up treasure in Heaven!"

Another friend of mine, Don Hiebert, will give tracts out at car washes, in waiting areas in restaurants, at a restaurant with a good tip, in bill payment envelopes and other strategic venues. Sometimes Don will ask a person, "Hi . . . are you interested in doing a short interview for a free $5 Starbucks Gift card?" Don then asks questions about life in general and then shifts to spiritual questions which lead into a gospel presentation.

Telemarketers

Has a telemarketer ever called you? I think they have called everyone. Many of the telemarketers that call me are from overseas in countries such as India or the Philippines. After they ask me several questions, I say to them, "Can I ask you a few questions?" They usually say yes, and then I ask them what country they are from; what religion they associate with, if any; and do they know for sure how to get to heaven. That gives me an opportunity to share the gospel with them. Many have thanked me for sharing how they can be sure they are going to heaven. Pastor David Jeremiah in his book *The*

Jesus You May Not Know tells of a friend who turns nuisance calls into good news calls. For example, if a caller is offering a vacation, his friend says, "I can't travel right now, but can I take a moment to tell you about the most exciting destination of all—heaven." Use your imagination for how to introduce the gospel to telemarketers.

Email Signature

Everyone has a signature at the end of their emails. I have added to my signature a video gospel presentation called "The Gift of Heaven" (https://jesusonline.com/receive-jesus/the-gift-of-heaven/) that clearly communicates how they can go to heaven. I want people to know that this is what I stand for. I may lose a few "sales" from letting people know about Christ, but I always want to get the message out, and the Lord will honor this. Let's not be ashamed of the gospel of Christ!

Instead of Tracts

At times, I have purchased for my church large quantities of *The Case for Easter* and *The Case for Christmas* by Lee Strobel, and *More Than a Carpenter* by Josh McDowell and Sean McDowell. The cost is very minimal. Books can be door openers for gospel conversations and be the seed in people's hearts to come to Christ in due time. I gave one of those books to my cardiologist who thanked me and said he would read it on the airplane. I have given out some of these books at the fitness gym. When I give one of them to a believer, I ask them to read it and then give it to a non-Christian friend. Recently, I had hip replacement surgery (yes, I am getting older) and gave out *More Than a Carpenter* books to my doctor, the physician assistant, the nurse and the anesthesiologist. Opportunities are everywhere.

How Some Churches Reach Out

George Barna of Barna Research found that most churches are interested in growing numerically by transfer growth but have a limited commitment to evangelism. Churches that have evangelism as a top priority typically have a senior pastor who has an intense desire to emphasize evangelism.

> Evangelist Bill Fay in his book *Share Jesus without Fear* wrote, "The primary mission of the church is to establish a way for every lost person to hear the news of salvation through faith in Jesus Christ."

There are myriad ways that churches reach out with the gospel. Here's a sampling of a few effective ways some churches reach the lost for Christ during the year.

Harvest Christian Fellowship in Riverside, California—Senior Pastor Greg Laurie constantly encourages people to come to Christ. One of their many ministries is a street witnessing ministry where a team goes out to the parks, cooks hot dogs, and shares Christ to the homeless and to soccer moms.

Canyon Hills Community Church, a megachurch in Bothell, Washington, has a Food Bank ministry in which they will distribute thousands of pounds of food to thousands of people of 11 ethnicities and nine different languages. They proactively share the gospel while providing food to families. Hundreds of people have received Christ since the inception of this ministry. They also have a "Damascus House" which is a gospel-centered drug and alcohol recovery ministry for men and women.

Here's a summary of their Evangelistic strategy at Canyon Hills:

- Their Community Life Groups commit to an ambassadorial lifestyle for spiritual growth and where evangelism is prioritized as a way of life in teaching all of Jesus (Matthew: 28:20)

- Their International Student Ministry with Bridges International of Cru encourages students to build relationships with international students.

- CHCC conducts a 10-week Evangelism Training and a 10-week Disciple Making training through the year.

- Every quarter, they sponsor a ½-day R3ACH Trainings focused on reaching religious demographics such as Hindus, Muslims, Buddhists, Hispanics, etc.

- They host Ramadan Dinner and Chai Chats in order to create opportunities to learn and have Gospel Conversations.

- High School students get trained and then go out applying what they have been trained on, planting seeds, praying for opportunities to have Gospel Conversations.

- Church-based Residency. Residents are trained in evangelism as a part of their Residency with Global Outreach

- Annually, they have a GO-week which focuses upon the Mission of God in Jesus and in us, as Jesus teaches twice (John 17:18, John 20:21) as the Father has sent me, I send you.

- Every Sunday morning at each of their four services, they have an altar call where people can come forward to talk to counselors about making a commitment to Christ.

Crossroads Bible Church in Bellevue, Washington, is a large, multi-ethnic church. For the last 10 years, a strong core of faithful Indian believers has mapped out most of the apartments on the east side of Seattle. Twice a month, they share Christ to the apartment residents and have handed out thousands of gospel tracts. They also share Christ in the community, at parks, in malls, at bus stations, and at festivals to engage in a gospel conversation with people.

Crossroads Community Church in Valencia, California has several outreach strategies lead by their Evangelism Pastor, Jim Stitzinger who shares the following:

- Scarlet Hope is a fantastic ministry that pursues women in the adult entertainment industry. Christian women are trained to evangelize those who are being exploited and trafficked. This ministry uses a technology service to text a gospel invitation to any of the over 40,000 women in Los Angeles that have made themselves known in this industry. They also provide home cooked meals on a weekly basis into various strip clubs, building conversations with the employees and presenting them with the gospel.

- Various Crossroads members have companies that produce a service or product that can be easily given away. From car wash gift certificates to jars of honey, they are able to take those donations and turn them into a springboard for the gospel. These items are given to the congregation, along with a church invitation, and then in turn given away throughout the community.

- The world of martial arts brings together a wide variety of people across our area. They started a "Jesus & Jiu-Jitsu" outreach Bible study to bring the good news of Christ to unbelievers that are interested in training together. This event usually starts with an hour of open mat training time followed by a Bible study lead by one of our pastors. While this is an unconventional gospel outreach, it is profoundly impactful!

- Another strategic ministry is "Hands of Hope." This gospel work brings compassionate believers into various retirement homes, to hold the hands and tell the gospel message to all who will hear. Understanding that retirement communities are often filled with lonely, discouraged people, it is a joy to see the good news of Jesus Christ bring hope to those who hear.

Scottsdale Bible Church in Scottsdale, Arizona, partners with several local nonprofit ministries designed to build relationship on an ongoing relational basis. Their Alpha groups (a nationwide evangelistic ministry) focuses on invitations to friends, family members, neighbors, and coworkers. Of the non-believers who attend, 70–90 percent come to Christ. There is a Beta class for anyone who desires to grow in Christ. For more information, go to https://scottsdalebible.com/events/alpha/. Alpha's national website at https://alphausa.org/run-alpha/ explains how to start an Alpha group.

Christ's Church of the Valley in greater Phoenix, Arizona, has several campuses. They equip their members with how to share their personal testimony and teach the gospel using the Romans Road or the Bridge Illustration. Thousands of families are involved in Stars Youth Sports program, and about half of the families don't initially attend church but later make Christ's Church of the Valley their church home.

Christ's Church in Gilbert, Arizona, reach out to the poor through their City Hope ministry where they provide food, clothing, and hygiene items which gives them an opportunity to share the love and gospel of Jesus Christ to those who don't know Christ.

Real Life Ministries in Post Falls, Idaho, started under Pastor Jim Putman with about 30 people and has grown to over 7,000 people based on multiplying small groups. They host several outreaches to the community such as a harvest festival and a Christmas outreach to needy kids. Go to https://resources.real-lifeministries.com *to see their resources.*

Shadow Mountain Community Church in San Diego, California, has several outreach ministries, including a food bank and a prison ministry. They equip their people for evangelism with Evangelism Explosion.

Family Church Network in West Palm Beach, Florida, has a vision to plant 100 churches in South Florida. The book *Turning Everyday Conversations into Gospel Conversations* shares highlights about multiplying disciples. The pastors of this church network aim to reach all six million South Floridians (Palm Beach, Broward, and Miami-Dade counties). Their strategy is to equip everyday, ordinary people to be missionaries in the places they live, work, and play.

Reaching Illegal Immigrants. *Many ministries and churches are reaching illegal immigrants who have come across US borders.* Samaritan's Purse and World Relief work with churches and evangelical partners to provide water, food, and other emergency supplies to illegal immigrants. Samaritan's Purse shares the gospel of Jesus Christ with them.

Door Hangers. A ministry called Prayandgo.com is engaged in a prayer walk and puts door hangers with the church's address, phone number, and email address for sending prayer requests.

Laundry Mat Evangelism. Some believers from a local church will take a ton of quarters and some baked goods and go to a local laundry mat and simply offer to pay for people's laundry. They seek to build relationships that will open up to spiritual conversations.

Street Evangelism. Steiger International has developed *Steiger Streets*, a handbook for street evangelism where adults go to places where young adults hang out to spark spiritual conversations. Their handbook is available at Steiger.org.

Here are some proven strategies for how to have an effective strategy for evangelism in your church:

1. Pray for the lost. Does your heart burn for lost people?

2. Inspire those in the church to be salt and light in your community.

3. Have an ongoing equipping class to teach church members how to share their faith.

4. Conduct mission trips or local outreaches where people share the gospel with others.

5. Have a follow-up system in place such as a Next Steps team member to meet with each new believer at a convenient time and place.

Pastor Charles Swindoll in his commentary on the Book of Romans reminds us of this:

We must care enough for the souls of others to go out of our way, to leave our comfort zones, to lay aside our desires in order to proclaim the gospel where it would not otherwise be heard. We must share the good news faithfully, freely, and often . . . we must submit their destinies to the loving care of their Creator. Pray that blind minds will see, and deaf souls will hear.

12

THE NEW ROMAN ROADS

When the Apostle Paul was led by the Holy Spirit to spread the gospel of Jesus Christ throughout the Roman Empire, his efforts were greatly facilitated by the network of Roman roads that covered 120,000 kilometers (almost 75,000 miles). God used these roads to spread the good news of Christ throughout the Roman Empire.

Jesus told His disciples that just prior to His return, "this gospel will be preached to all nations" (Matthew 24:14 NIV). How could this be possible unless God raised up a new technology that would enable the gospel to reach every person on earth? Little did they realize that 2,000 years later, God would raise up a new Roman road that would lead to the literal fulfillment of Jesus's words.

Just as the gospel was spread throughout the Roman roads during the birth of Christianity, so today the gospel is being spread worldwide by the Internet. As of this writing in 2024, there are 5.35 billion global Internet users of this new Roman road. That number is expected to reach 6.54 billion in 2025 primarily through the proliferation of smartphones.

Easier and Faster Ways of Communicating

At the click of a mouse on a computer or a tap on a smartphone, the gospel can be sent out in seconds around the world and in different languages. We are in a new digital era where almost everything is done digitally, and technology is affecting the spread of the good news all over the world.

Easy Understanding of Scripture and Gospel Resources

Because of technological changes, people can obtain gospel and biblical materials even in remote areas where they were previously unavailable. The gospel is being spread worldwide through this new technology of the Internet.

Many ministries are using this new Roman road to fulfill Jesus's Great Commission to take the gospel worldwide before He returns.

JesusOnline Ministries is one such ministry that has been proclaiming the gospel on the Internet since 2005 and has reached nearly every nation of the world.

JesusOnline Ministries

JesusOnline Ministries (JOM) has received over a quarter of a billion website visits from people in 195 countries who have read the articles or watched videos about Jesus's life, crucifixion, and resurrection. For each person who indicates a decision for Christ, the cost to the website is incredibly low at less than one dollar.

JesusOnline Ministries uses a proven four-step outreach strategy to reach them with the truth about Jesus.

Step 1. JOM poses questions people are asking about Jesus. They identify those with an online search history related to questions they're asking about God, Jesus, faith, and the Bible.

Step 2. People click ads that link them to compelling gospel articles and videos. By placing curiosity-provoking ads on thousands of promising websites every day, JOM captures interest and makes people think about who this Jesus is that they have heard about.

Step 3. Visitors to the website then discover answers that reveal Jesus's true identity and the life He offers. After hearing the gospel on video or in print, they discover that Jesus is their Savior and Lord and have the opportunity to come to Him by faith.

Step 4. JOM follows up with those who respond and encourages them to join the JO App community where a discipleship pastor and team of volunteers help members nurture their relationship with Jesus. The team also prays for people and helps guide individuals to find biblical answers for their challenges.

The three main websites are Y-Jesus.com, Jesusonline.com, and Jesusonlineministries.com.

Y-Jesus has PDF articles and videos on such topics as "Is Jesus God?" "Did Jesus Rise from the Dead? (also, a video version); "Has Science Discovered God?" "The Gift of Heaven" (in PDF and video formats), and a host of other topics. These articles and videos can be placed on Facebook or Instagram, or emailed to your non-Christian friends with whom you are sharing the gospel. I have sent some of these articles and videos to non-Christians who are looking for reasons to believe and have also posted these articles on Facebook.

Jesusonlineministries.org shares the vision of JOM along with "The Gift of Heaven" video that has reached millions of viewers with hundreds of thousands making a decision for Christ.

JesusOnline.com has an app downloaded by millions called the **JOApp**. This app has resources such as Bible studies, gospel tracts, online Bibles, New Adventure with Jesus, and several other resources.

In 2023, JOM had 98,393 daily visits, 6,625 daily decisions, and 2,418,015 people who committed their lives to follow Jesus from 190 countries around the world. Over 300,000 of these decisions were from "The Gift of Heaven" video that reached people even in many countries where Christians are persecuted.

2030 Ministry Vision:

- One billion website all-time visits

- 30 million all-time decisions for Christ

Below are brief samplings of the thousands of comments JOM receives on a monthly basis.

Moges, Ethiopia

I was thinking to kill myself. I was in depression and stress, and I think I'm alone and everybody hates me, but Jesus told me if you're alone I am with you. If anyone doesn't love you, I love you and he is my friend and my father. I can't describe his love to me.

Roberto, Guatemala

I've been an atheist for a long time. I asked God to show me if He was real. But last month I began fearing about death and asked God to show me if He was real. I prayed and asked Him for a sign to help me know the truth. Then I was navigating on Pinterest, and your ad came about the resurrection. Although I wasn't searching for anything about life after death, I realized this was God's answer, and I read the article showing that Jesus really rose. I'm glad that God answered me. Thank you for your website.

Kalyani, India

I am a Hindu who was told the truth of Christ very recently. . . . I have seen and heard enough to believe in Jesus, but my nagging mind plagued me with doubts, and I ended up on this wonderful site. Such direct, amazing facts. Verifiable, source-cited. You people don't know how much it helps me to read these articles. How much it calms me. Keep up the good job. Hope this site helps many lost sheep reach the truth. God bless.

Reynaldo, Israel

I am now truly convinced that Jesus and God truly exist . . . and His promises are true . . . I like to devote my life to Him. . . . Amen!

Serwaa, Ghana

Could you believe I was crying before I clicked on the link? I'm in debt to the extent of thinking of taking my life for everything to end. I have a seven-month-old baby girl too. And now I have seen how wrong I am thinking I have nobody to help me, Almighty God is here for me.

Ahmed, Ghana

Although I've been a Muslim for 10 years, I read your article and am very grateful for your insightful facts about Jesus. I'm really inspired how your website helped me discover the truth of the gospel.

Pastor Ayodele, Nigeria

I am a minister of the gospel for over 30 years now, but I have never seen the gospel so clearly presented as this. This message will help us present the gospel message better. Thank you.

Neil, Philippines

This article really captures my heart, my whole being. . . . It makes me cry out loud alone in my room. . . . I feel sorry for all my sins.

Sakeena, Pakistan

It was amazing. I never read such content. May God accept me with my sins.

Michael, New Guinea

Convincing and heart touching, and this is my turning point. My tears rolled down my eyes while praying the prayer. I need to return to Jesus Christ, the Son of the living God. Eternal life is real, and Jesus Christ is the firstborn into the eternal life.

Miguel, Venezuela

Until today I never understood why God gave His only Son as a sacrifice for us who literally do not deserve it. I cannot imagine giving my son for other people. That's how great God's love is, and today more than ever, my God, I love you, and I receive you.

Ariel, Colombia

Now I understand that Jesus Christ is the one who will help me fill that void in my life. I receive Him in my heart and my life and accept Him as owner and master of my life. I ask you, Jesus, to come in and take control of my being and make me what you want me to be. Amen. For a long time, I was looking for you, but I did not see until today.

Beverly, Guyana

I was deeply moved by these wonderful words of life today. I feel that I found a new life. I am moved to live my life with Jesus. I found this new birth with tears in my eyes. These words touched my soul, and I think I am now free to live my true life and have that relationship with God.

Abdel, Peru

It has helped me to understand many new things. I am grateful, and I do not consider it a coincidence to find this spiritual help. I was a convinced atheist, but I had the opportunity to meet God.

Alexander, Canada

I now believe in God; I finally have faith. Sweet Jesus, I love you. You're everything to us. It's true. I acknowledge Your sacrifice of Your life for us!

Rosario, Mexico

I've had some questions about Jesus's resurrection, but now I see it so clearly. He rose again, to the tears that now run down my cheeks. He resurrected. Thank you very much.

Kathleen, USA

This is the most wonderful article I have ever read. Being raised Catholic, it never crossed my mind that Jesus is my Lord and He rose up to heaven so we could have eternal life with Him. And that I pray for.

Enrico, Italy

I was having a crisis of faith, and suddenly I got this link where I found so much benefit. Jesus sought me out, and I accepted Him.

Zhimoka, India

I am struggling to get out of addiction and sinful habits. This article indeed has helped me answer my questions and doubts about whether a person like me can be given a chance in life. Now I believe I can because Jesus is indeed my Savior and my one true God.

Sujatha, India

I am a Hindu, but while reading about Jesus I am crying. I don't know why, but after reading your article, I feel peace in my heart. I accept Jesus as my saviour. Thank you very much.

Youcef, Algeria

Now I have evidence that Jesus died on the cross and three days later He resurrected from death. In spite of my precedent belief as a Muslim that Jesus never died on the Cross, today I feel free on discovering the reality about the Christ thanks to so wonderful evidence. Life without Jesus is not worth living."

Global Media Outreach (GMO) is another effective ministry that leverages technology to reach the world for Christ. GMO has seen millions receive Christ worldwide since it began. In summary, several ministries such as JesusOnline Ministries are taking the Lord's words seriously and using the new Roman road of the Internet to proclaim the gospel to every nation.

Articles and Videos to Share Christ

You can go to Y-Jesus.com and send an article or video to those you are witnessing to and ask them their opinion for further follow-up.

You can also post the gospel or an apologetic article on Facebook, Instagram, or other social media about the Lord and how Christ has changed your life.

The Social Media Phenomenon

The gospel remains the same, but the methods change. Today, social media platforms such as Facebook, Twitter, Instagram, TikTok, YouTube, LinkedIn, Snapchat, Pinterest, and Reddit are reaching billions of people daily. Facebook is the world's largest social network. As of January 2024, Facebook had 3.05 billion monthly active users (MAU). It's the most used, most universal, and most effective social media tool for evangelism. The vast majority of users are between 25 and 54 years of age.

YouTube has 2.5 billion MAU; Instagram has 2 billion MAU. More than 80 percent of every generation uses social media at least once per day.

First Chronicles 12:32 says, "Of the sons of Issachar, men who understood the times, with knowledge of what Israel should do."

The Internet and social media present an amazing opportunity to get the gospel out to the world. Thousands of evangelists are using social media platforms to spread the gospel.

Here are some ways to use social media to share the gospel.

1. Understand your audience and the social media platform you want to reach. With Facebook, tap the circle to the right of the audience you'd like to see your content

(example: friends, public, only me). Thirty percent or more of people between the ages of 18 and 24 make up most Instagram users. To post on Instagram, you can turn on your Facebook account in the share section. The share to section will be set to your Instagram account. For public accounts, anyone on Instagram can see your posts.

2. In general, ages 20 to 29 are the biggest users of social media.

3. Pray for people viewing your post. Ask for prayer requests. "How can I pray for you and follow up for an update?" Share prayers and praises.

4. Share your story or personal testimony, scripture, and what it means to you. Share posts from your church. Share burdens. Share resources to meet needs. Share opportunities to connect. Share the gospel message and how to know Christ.

5. Post regularly because over time the message of the gospel will penetrate a person's heart. Be consistent.

6. Respond to comments you may receive. Follow-up is important, and over time a person may come to Christ since it takes

time for people to understand and receive the gospel.

7. Many pastors post their sermons on the Internet and social media. David Jeremiah's ministry Turning Point is available on most all social media platforms, including Facebook, Instagram, and TikTok. His organization informed me recently that they have reached more than 300 million organically on these platforms in a short period of time.

8. R. York Moore, President and CEO of the Coalition of Christian Outreach and Tellthestory.net, posts three to five short videos a day, mainly on basic doctrines of sin, judgment, and common struggles such as pornography, anxiety, and fear, as well as what salvation is and how a person is saved. Moore uses TikTok as a social media platform and has been doing that for two years. He says that the most effective platforms for getting the gospel out are TikTok, YouTube Shorts, and Instagram Reels. As of November 2023, Moore's sites have 717,000 followers, over 8 million hitting his posts, and an estimated 400,000 people who have received Christ. Moore commented, "God is using TikTok in a powerful way to reach Gen Z

with the gospel." He suggested using www. robertbenjaminconsulting.com to learn how to use social media.

9. Search on Instagram or YouTube on topics such as faith in Jesus, apologetics, sermons, evangelism, salvation, the resurrection of Jesus, the second coming, and other topics. You will get a host of posts.

Edigital ministries such as www.godkulture.global. com, www.udemy.com, and www.delmethod.com explain how to use social media to share the gospel. You can also contact someone in your church who is tech savvy and ask them to show you how to use social media to share Christ evangelistically.

SeekGrowLove.com says, "Internet evangelism is how the nations will have an opportunity to hear and receive the good news. . . . Today one person, right out of the comfort of his home, can reach millions of people in places he has never been and most likely, never will go. . . . As good stewards, we must use what God has given us if we desire to obey the Great Commission and bring the return of our anticipated Savior!"

13

ANSWERING OBJECTIONS

What Is Apologetics?

In the book *Therefore Stand,* Wilbur Smith defines apologetics as "a verbal defense, a speech in defense of what one has done or a truth which one believes."

First Peter 3:15 says, "But sanctify Christ as Lord in your hearts, always being ready to make a defense to everyone who asks you to give an account for the hope that is in you, yet with gentleness and reverence." The Greek word *apologia* means "a speech of defense."

Theologian John Stott said, "We cannot pander to a man's intellectual arrogance, but we must cater to his intellectual integrity."

I once shared Christ with a person who was studying for a doctoral degree in psychology. I gave him some evidence on the resurrection of Christ and of Jesus being God by showing him that Jesus was either a liar, a lunatic, or Lord and that it makes far greater sense to believe that Jesus is who He claimed to be (Lord, God). The man said he had never heard answers like this before, and I often wonder if later on he made a profession of faith in Christ. Our aim is to make the gospel clear and answer people's questions as best we know how.

A Different Worldview

"For the word of the cross is foolishness to those who are perishing, but to us who are saved, it is the power of God" (1 Corinthians 1:18). Expect people who have not been brought up in a church or have never read the Bible to have a different worldview than yours.

How to Give an Answer

You don't have to know all the answers to every question. If someone asks a question you don't know the answer to, be honest, and tell them you don't know. Then say, "Let me research this, and let's get together again for coffee to discuss it." That could lead to more dialogue. Invite the person to read a book such as

The Case for Faith by Lee Strobel. Our main goal is to introduce the person to Christ, and that may take many conversations and a lot of time.

Tim Muehlhoff, a professor at Biola University and author of *I Beg to Differ: Navigating Difficult Conversations with Truth and Love,* suggests asking yourself four questions when sharing with people who may be averse to Christianity or the Bible.

1. Exactly **what** does this person believe?
2. **Why** does this person believe what they believe?
3. **Where** do we agree?
4. Based on this knowledge, **how** should I proceed, or what is the one thing I should say?

Aaron Pierce in *Not Beyond Reach* recommends following this process: affirm, reframe, challenge.

- **Affirm** whatever is true or admirable about the person's viewpoint.

- **Reframe** their viewpoint and point out any false assumptions.

- **Challenge** the untruths that stand in the way of the gospel.

Win the Relationship

You can never argue anyone into the kingdom of God. It may be that the person is a tire-kicker and just wants a friendship or wants to see if Christ is displayed in your life.

At some point in your discussion with someone, you might ask them, "What would it take for you to receive Christ into your life?" or "What is holding you back from receiving Christ?"

You may be surprised at their answers. It could be something simple or a misconception about the Bible or the Christian faith.

Ignorance

Often people who raise questions have either never heard the gospel or their ignorance is self-imposed. When the Apostle Paul preached to the Athenians on Mars Hill in Acts 17, some of his audience believed, but some did not and then mocked Paul. As the old saying goes, the same sun that hardens clay softens butter.

Lean into Disagreement

Sam Chan, author of *How to Talk about Jesus*, recommends leaning into disagreement because being vulnerable to disagreement shows unconditional love. Jesus often ate and drank with people who disagreed with Him. The gospel by its very nature is offensive because people will react to the notion of sin and their need to repent.

Avoid Endless Rabbit Trails

If people you share Christ with keep bombarding you with questions, you could ask them, "If I answer that question, would you be ready to receive Christ as your Lord and Savior?"

Greg Laurie said, "People will try to take you down endless rabbit trails . . . but the main thing is to keep the main thing the main thing which is the gospel faithfully delivered."

When Lee Strobel encounters a skeptic, he suggests that they do a cost-benefit analysis. He tells them to take a sheet of paper and list what Christ offers on one side—forgiveness, peace of mind, eternal life, fulfillment, power to live the Christian life, and so on. On the other side, he asks them to list their current lifestyle—lack of purpose, no peace, no pardon, no power, eternal separation from God, and so on. He wants to show them the difference so they can see what Christ offers compared to what they are experiencing. That can be a good exercise to give to someone who is hopefully searching despite their smokescreens.

"We use God's mighty weapons, not worldly weapons to knock down the strongholds of human reasoning and to destroy false arguments" (2 Corinthians 10:4 NLT).

What about Scoffers?

Jesus warned against those who treat the gospel with scorn. "Do not give what is holy to dogs, and do not throw your pearls before swine, or they will trample them under their feet, and turn and tear you to pieces" (Matthew 7:6).

Some people, no matter how much evidence you give them, will choose not to believe (John 3:19; Romans 1:21, 2:5). Case in point is Judas who saw Jesus perform countless miracles, heard amazing teaching, and yet denied the Lord. It took Noah, a preacher of righteousness, 120 years to build the ark, and only his family turned to the Lord. Jesus said, "For the coming of the Son of Man will be just like the days of Noah" (Matthew 24:37).

Don't get discouraged if people reject your gospel presentation. Our responsibility is to declare the good news of salvation regardless of how people respond to it. The only hope for a scoffer is the healing touch of the Holy Spirit who can open their blind eyes to the gospel.

In Luke 14, Jesus shares the parable of the dinner. Many who were invited gave excuses and did not come. Finally, "the master said to the slave, 'Go out into the highways and along the hedges, and compel them to come in, so that my house may be filled. For I tell you, none of those men who were invited shall taste of my dinner.'" (Luke 14:23–24). This is a picture of God the Father wanting us to urge non-believers to come to Christ so they will participate in the glories of heaven forever. We must urge them to respond to the Father's invitation and then leave the results in God's hands.

Reasons People Object to the Gospel

Moral Issue

People's basic problem ultimately is not intellectual. It's moral. "But the natural man does not accept the things of the Spirit of God, for they are foolishness to him; and he cannot understand them, because they are spiritually appraised" (1 Corinthians 2:14).

I witnessed to a guy who kept bringing up objections to the gospel. Finally, he asked me what the Bible said about premarital sex and abortion. I found out later that he had gotten his girlfriend pregnant, and she had had an abortion. I was honest about premarital sex and abortion being wrong but focused on what happens when we receive Christ—He forgives us and cleanses us of all sin.

Paul Little once wrote, "Alleged intellectual problems are often a smokescreen covering moral rebellion."

The famous atheist Aldous Huxley wrote, "For myself, as no doubt for most of my friends . . . we objected to the morality because it interfered with our sexual freedom."

Emotional Issue

I shared the gospel with a young lady who said she was an atheist. When I asked her how the universe came into being, she admitted that the main reason she rejected a belief in God was because her mother had tried to slam religion down her throat. She had an emotional issue with her mom. Prior to coming to Christ, many atheists such as Lee Strobel and Josh McDowell had emotional barriers.

Pride and the Will

In John 7:17 (ESV), Jesus said, "If anyone is willing to do God's will, he will know whether the teaching is from God or whether I am speaking on my own authority."

The reason most educated people don't believe is the same reason most uneducated people don't believe. They don't want to believe. Randy Newman in his book *Bringing the Gospel Home* states that when Jesus spoke to the religious Jews, He said, "Because I tell you the truth, you do not believe me" (John 8:45 NIV). He did not say "although I tell you the truth." The religious Jews failed to believe because they had a pride issue.

Years ago, I gave a book on the evidence for Christ to an atheist airline stewardess. She responded, "Dave, thank you for your kindness. I am returning this book to you. Pass it on to someone who might like it. I'm afraid I am hopeless to change my opinion." Part of my reply to her was this: "God will never impose His will on anyone. There may be reasons why you have chosen not to seek God, but we're all getting older, and someday you and even I may find ourselves staring death in the face— whether through health issues or even an accident. My counsel to you is to ask the Lord to come into your life, to forgive you, and to give you eternal life.

The most famous verse in the Bible says, 'For God so loved the world that He gave His only begotten Son that whoever believes in Him will not perish but have everlasting life.' You may be passionate about the government, but I am passionate about the awesome privilege of having a personal relationship with the Lord. People are often incapable of solving real needs. I would rather you express how you feel than not. God bless."

Idols

The rich young ruler asked Jesus: "Good Teacher, what shall I do so that I may inherit eternal life?" Jesus told him to sell all his possessions and give to the poor. The rich young ruler "Went away grieving; for he was one who owned much property" (Mark 10:17, 22).

People have various idols in their life. I emailed Mark Cahill, author of *One Heartbeat Away*, regarding his witness efforts to Tiger Woods and Michael Jordan and their need for Christ. Mark wrote back, "Amazing how money, wealth, and fame can make someone put God in the back seat." The well-known athlete Deion Sanders had tried everything—parties, women, expensive jewelry—but had no peace and was on the verge of suicide before he found Christ.

Know Why You Believe

We need to know why we believe what we believe. There are many reasons why the Christian faith makes total sense, but ultimately it comes down to a personal encounter with Jesus and the empty tomb.

Paul Little in his classic book *Know Why You Believe* makes this profound statement: "'Little, how do you know you haven't been taken in by a colossal propaganda program? After all, you can't see God, touch him, taste him, or feel him.' And then I go on to ask myself how I know the gospel is true. I always come back to two basic factors: the objective, external, historical facts of the resurrection, and the subjective, internal, personal experience of Christ that I have."

God Is Patient

Chuck Swindoll said, "When you think you know someone who is too far gone to believe in Christ, remember the centurion. If that hardened, tough-minded Roman soldier could become aware of the truth, so can your lost loved one." When the centurion saw Christ die on the cross, he said, "Truly this was the Son of God!" (Matthew 27:54).

I encourage you to do your own research for the answers to some of the questions people commonly ask.

14

ANSWERING SPECIFIC OBJECTIONS

I'm an Atheist

An atheist believes that nothing × nobody = everything.

Sam Chan recommends Tim Keller's book *Making Sense of God* because it focuses on the reasons we need to believe in the existence of God.

Anthony Flew, probably the most respected atheist of the last 100 years, changed from atheism after studying DNA and said, "I now believe that the universe was brought into existence by an infinite Intelligence. I believe that this universe's intricate laws manifest what scientists have called the Mind of God."

Norman Geisler's book *I Don't Have Enough Faith to Be an Atheist* wrote, "If there is no God, why is there something rather than nothing at all?

Years ago, I was canvassing a neighborhood for a new church plant. I knocked on the door of a home and introduced myself. The man at the front door stated, "We're atheists. We don't believe in God. Just make God appear right now on the front lawn, and I'll believe. Go ahead, make Him appear!" I replied, "The universe is 15 billion light years in all directions, and you're a dot in the universe. Is it possible that God could exist outside your realm of experience?" And he said yes. Then I said, "You're not an atheist. You'd be an agnostic, and there are two kinds of agnostics. One says, 'I don't know, and I don't care.' The other one says, 'I don't know, but I'm willing to find out.' Which one are you?" He said, "I don't know, but I'm willing to find out." I noticed that his countenance had dropped from one of arrogance to one of astonishment and humility. I began to share the gospel with him, but his common law wife (the neighbors at the next door I knocked on told me they weren't married) behind the door yelled, "Honey, it's dinner time," so I was unable to finish sharing the gospel with him. I gave him a tract, and I often wonder to this day if he ever pondered what I shared with him and if later on he came to Christ.

William Craig, an American philosopher and Christian apologist, has five powerful arguments for God and Christianity. I'll use the acronym CAUSE.

C—CAUSE: Whatever begins to exist has a cause. The universe began to exist; therefore, the universe has a cause. Either no one created something out of nothing, or someone created something out of nothing. If you can't believe that nothing caused something, then you don't have enough faith to be an atheist.

A—ACCURACY: Design of the universe defies coincidence and shows there is an Intelligent Designer. Every design had a designer. The universe is highly complex in its design. Stephen Hawking wrote, "If the rate of expansion one second after the big bang had been smaller by even one part in a hundred thousand million million, the universe would have re-collapsed before it ever reached its present size." The universe had a Designer.

U—UNIVERSAL MORALITY is evidence that there is a God. There must be a God to account for the sense of right and wrong that is universal to humankind.

S—SUBJECTIVE EXPERIENCE is that God can be known by those who seek Him. Your personal testimony is proof that God can be known and exists.

E—EMPTY TOMB and eyewitness accounts. Many atheists such as Josh McDowell, Lee Strobel, Simon Greenleaf, Frank Morison, and others became Christians by studying the resurrection of Christ. Go to https://y-jesus.com/ wwrj/6-jesus-rise-dead/ to watch the video or read the article.

What About Those Who Have Never Heard about Jesus?

A guy named Mark mentioned to me that he had asked several people a question that no one could answer. Here was his question: "What about those who have never heard the gospel before? God won't send them to hell, will he?" I could tell by the expression on his face after I answered his question that he had never heard the answer before. His ignorance, which was really arrogance, was self-imposed. He didn't want to believe. He wanted to continue in his sinful lifestyle.

This question calls into question the justice and fairness of God. There are books, videos, and articles on this question, but the way I answer this question is by using the acrostic **JUSTICE.**

J—GOD IS JUST: Whatever God does, He does fairly and with perfect justice. Genesis 18:25 (NKJV) says, "Shall not the Judge of all the earth do right?" People in general want justice. We all want justice, and when history comes to an end, everyone will see how perfect God's justice is.

U—GOD'S LOVE IS UNCONDITIONAL and infinite. First John 4:8, says, "God is love." He "desires all men to be saved" (1 Timothy 2:4). God longs for people to come to repentance and to return to Him. He wants heaven to be populated. "He is patient with you, not wanting anyone to perish, but everyone to come to repentance" (2 Peter 3:9 NIV).

S—GOD HAS SHOWN all men that He exists by **creation** (Romans 1:19–20; Psalm 19:1–4) and by **conscience** (Romans 2:14–15; 1:19; John 1:9). Every person born into this world knows that there is a God by external means (creation) and by internal witness (their conscience). Every culture has a belief in gods or God. But what do people do with this knowledge that God exists? Most people suppress the truth of God (Romans 1:18–19).

T—TRANSGRESSED TERMS: Every person has sinned before a holy God in thought, word, and deed (Romans 3:23; James 2:10; Romans 3:10–12; James 4:17; Isaiah 64:6). They have also violated the moral standard written in their hearts, which is why their conscience bothers them when they violate that moral law. All stand guilty before the holy God of the universe.

I—INITIATE (CALL UPON) GOD): The Bible tells us that if a person wholeheartedly seeks God, they will find him. "You will seek Me and find Me when you search for Me with all your heart" (Jeremiah 29:13). Before Jesus came to earth, Abraham, Rahab, and others in the Old Testament put their faith in the one true God and His provision for their sins (Genesis 15:6; Joshua 2:9–11). God will move heaven and earth to see that a person comes to know God if they will earnestly seek Him.

In Dreams and Visions: Is Jesus Awakening the Muslim World? Tom Doyle shows how many Muslims are coming to Christ through spectacular dreams. The wise men in Matthew 2:1–12 followed the light God gave them (the star) and brought them to the Christ child. In Acts

10, Peter and Cornelius both had dreams, and Cornelius' whole household came to Christ.

C—JESUS IS THE CATEGORICAL CURE: Jesus is the only way to salvation (John 14:6; Acts 4:12). People before Christ put their faith in a Messiah who would ultimately die for their sins. We look back to the death, burial, and resurrection of Christ as having paid for our sins on the cross.

E—EXPECT EXAMINATION: When you witness to a person who has clearly heard the gospel, the God of the universe will not ask them, "What about those who have never heard?" Rather, the Lord will show them the many ways He has tried to get their attention and will ask them, "What have you done with my Son, Jesus, who died for you and has paid the full price for your sins?"

Is Jesus Christ God?

Jesus never acquiesced to the idea that He was simply a great moral teacher.

Jesus Claimed to Be God

Many times, Jesus claimed to be God, the Creator of the universe. He said to Philip, "Whoever has seen Me, has seen the Father" (John 14:9 ESV).

Jesus claimed to be the great "I AM" (John 8:58), which infuriated the Jewish leaders of His day, and they sought to kill Him "because you, a mere man, have made yourself God" (John 10:33). His power over nature, disease, and death (Mark 4:41; John 9:1–41) proved He was God.

Jesus Predicted His Resurrection from the Dead

No other great religious leader dared to predict that he would rise from the dead (John 2:19; John 11:25–26).

Examining the Alternatives

- **Liar:** How could the greatest moral teacher who ever lived be the greatest deceiver of all time, even among his closest friends?

- **Lunatic:** Psychologists state that Jesus had the most stable personality ever. When Jesus was being crucified, He exhibited great composure and poise, and uttered these words: "Father forgive them for they know not what they are doing" (Luke 23:34).

- **Legend:** The overwhelming evidence from history both by secular historians and Christian scholars is that Jesus was an historical figure of great significance.

- **Lord:** That Jesus is Lord is backed up by His life, incredible teachings, miracles, and resurrection.

Did Jesus Rise from the Dead?

Evidence of Christ's Death. Gregory Koukl in *The Story of Reality* indicates that the vast majority of scholars, including those who are entirely secular, agree that Jesus died on a Roman cross on a Friday, that He was buried in a tomb, and that the tomb was empty on Sunday morning. Numerous witnesses testified that they saw Jesus alive multiple times.

Early Accounts. The earliest creed taken from 1 Corinthians 15:3–4 alludes to the death, burial, and resurrection of Christ. It has been dated within months of Christ's death.

Empty Tomb. All the enemies of Christ had to do to destroy Christianity was simply to produce the body of Christ, which they never did. Christ's tomb remains empty. Theologian R. C. Sproul said, "Buddha is dead. Mohammad is dead. Moses is dead. Confucius is dead. But . . . Christ is alive."

Eyewitnesses. Besides the four Gospels, there are non-biblical sources that reference the resurrection of Christ (e.g., Tacitus, Pliny the Younger, Josephus, Lucian).

Experience of Christ. Every believer, the moment they receive Christ, are indwelt by Jesus (Colossians 1:27). Jesus says in Revelation 3:20 (ESV), "Behold, I stand at the door and knock. If anyone hears my voice and opens the door [of their heart], I will come into him and eat with him, and he with me."

Why Do People Suffer?

Greek philosopher Epicurus who lived a few hundred years before Christ proposed this argument:

1. God is all-good and all-powerful.
2. An all-good God would want there to be no evil.
3. An all-powerful God would have the power to eradicate evil.
4. There is evil.
5. Therefore, God is not both all-good and all-powerful.

A good answer to this argument can be found in Lee Strobel's book *The Case for Faith* where he quotes philosopher Peter Kreeft that evil is evidence for God:

"If there is no God, where did we get the standard of goodness by which we judge evil as evil?" God created the possibility of evil. Man's freedom is the source of evil. God could decree by midnight all evil cease, but by 12:01 a.m., none of us would be left. Someday God will destroy all evil.

In his book *The Case for Christ*, Lee Strobel wrote that God has "demonstrated how the very worst thing that has ever happened in the history of the world ended up resulting in the very best thing that has ever happened in the history of the world" (the death of God on the cross).

Isn't the Christian Experience Only a Psychological Crutch?

Conversions Contrast

Paul Little in *Know Why You Believe* states, "We cannot explain Christian experience on a conditioned reflex basis . . . since thousands reared in Christian homes unfortunately never become Christians. . . . In Christianity, our personal subjective experience is tied into the objective historical fact of the resurrection of Christ." Some people who were raised in a Christian home later abdicated their faith, whereas many who had no exposure at all to Christ became followers of Christ. Christianity is not based on wish fulfillment;

it is based on the objective historical fact that Jesus rose from the dead.

Christ Is Constant

Over 60 generations have shown that Jesus changes lives. We are created for God. St. Augustine said, "You have made us for yourself, O Lord, and our heart is restless until it rests in you."

The ultimate answer to the argument of wish fulfillment or that Christianity is a psychological crutch is that our experience with Christ is that it is based on irrefutable, objective facts—the resurrection of Jesus Christ from the dead. See the video and article "Did Jesus Rise from the Dead" (Y-Jesus.com).

Is the Bible the Word of God?

Here are some of the answers to this question:

Argument from Analogy

God has instituted communication in the natural world. Therefore, it seems probable that communication from God to man would take place.

Argument from the Indestructibility of the Bible

The Bible is the best preserved of all books transmitted from antiquity. The Bible has been preserved despite attempts to destroy it and deny it.

Argument from the Character of the Bible

The contents of the Bible are unsurpassed in its subjects (creation, sin, trinity, etc.). The Bible was written by 40 authors over 1,500 years but clearly the product of one Author (2 Timothy 3:16; 2 Peter 1:20–21).

Argument from the Influence of the Bible

The Bible has had a scientific, cultural, social, political, and domestic influence. It has answers to the major questions of philosophy such as "Why does evil exist? What is good and right?"

Argument from Fulfilled Prophecy

One-fourth of the Bible is prophetic. Jesus fulfilled over 300 specific prophecies (Psalm 22; Isaiah 52, 53), and the Bible gives a panorama of future events with many prophecies that have already been fulfilled (Matthew 24; Revelation).

Argument from the Claims of Scripture

Over 3,000 times, the Bible declares itself the Word of God and having divine authorship. Aristotle said that a book is innocent until proven guilty.

Argument from the Scientific Accuracy of the Bible

The Bible says that the stars in the heavens are innumerable (Jeremiah 33:22). Scientists in the past thought there were only a few thousand stars in the universe, but recent scientific discoveries reveal millions of galaxies with hundreds of millions of stars.

Until the 19th century, physicians bled a patient, hoping that would heal them. But the Bible all along stated that blood is the source of life (Leviticus 17:11).

In his book *Scientific Facts in the Bible*, Ray Comfort lists 100 scientific facts.

Won't a Good, Moral Life Get Me to Heaven?

If someone asks this question, ask them if they ever told a lie, stole something, took the Lord's name in vain, looked at someone of the opposite sex in a lustful way, and so on. Every person has broken God's commandments (James 2:10; Matthew 5:48; Romans 3:10, 23).

Acknowledge that you as well as they have sinned, but the difference is that you have found forgiveness in Christ. "For all have sinned and fall short of the glory of God" (Romans 3:23).

You may be a great swimmer, but none of us could swim to Hawaii. We'd all fall short. People often don't receive Christ because they won't believe, not because they can't believe.

Nicodemus: In John 3, Nicodemus, a Pharisee and member of the Sanhedrin in Israel, comes to Jesus, who tells him, "Truly, truly, I say to you, unless one is born again, he cannot see the kingdom of God" (John 3:3). Faith in Jesus Christ, the One who paid the penalty of sin, is how a person is born again. It is trusting in Jesus Christ alone, repenting of sin, and receiving Him as your Savior and Lord. None of Nicodemus' good deeds could earn him a place in heaven. By the end of the Gospel of John, Nicodemus appears to have become a disciple of Christ.

The Thief on the Cross: The thief on the cross said to Jesus, "'Remember me when you come into your Kingdom.' Jesus said to him, 'Truly, I say to you, today you will be with me in paradise'" (Luke 23:43). He entered into heaven solely on the mercy and grace of God, just like everyone else who puts their faith in Christ. Jesus paid for our sins at the cross and offers us the free gift of His righteousness (2 Corinthians 5:21).

Why Would a Loving God Send Someone to Hell?

You could reverse this question by asking, "If God is so holy, why would He ever let anyone into heaven?" The Bible is very clear. God says: "I take no pleasure in the death of the wicked, but rather that the wicked turn from his way and live" (Ezekiel 33:11). The cross of Christ shows God's desire that people can receive His grace and forgiveness and spend eternity in heaven as opposed to hell.

When people ask how a loving God can send a person to hell, Sam Chan asks them to read with him Jesus's parable of the rich man and Lazarus (Luke 16:19–31). He then asks them what they like about the story and what it says about hell. He says that people often think the rich man justly deserves to be in hell. C. S. Lewis wrote, "The door of hell is locked on the inside." There are only two kinds of people— those who say to God, "Thy will be done" and those to whom God in the end says, "Thy will be done." All that are in hell ultimately choose it.

The Bible is Full of Errors, and There Are So Many Translations

If someone says, "The Bible is full or errors," ask them to show you one. Chances are they have never read the Bible and can't point to a single so-called error. If they say, "There are so many translations," implying that the Bible can't be trusted, the simple answer is that all translations come from the Hebrew (Old Testament) and Greek (New Testament), and they all say basically the same thing. Ask them, "Do you mind if I share with you what the main theme of the Bible is and how it changed my life?" Then share the gospel and/or your personal testimony with them.

What About Other Religions?

All religions other than Christianity exhort people to reach God by their own efforts with no assurance of eternal life or heaven. They can be summed up in one word—**Do**. Even Mohammad, the founder of Islam, did not know what Allah would do to him after he died (Quran 46:9). If Mohammad had no assurance of salvation, what hope is there for his followers?

Christianity is based on one word—**Done**. Jesus paid for all our sins at the cross (Gal. 2:16). By accepting Jesus and His death on our behalf, we are justified and made righteous before a holy God. Jesus staked His full claims to deity on His resurrection. Today, Jesus's tomb is empty. Buddha, Mohammed, Confucius—their tombs are occupied. Only Jesus claimed to be God incarnate and the only way to heaven. Jesus said, "I am the way, the truth and the life; no one comes to the Father but through Me" (John 14:6).

I'm Not Ready

Ask someone, "What is the reason you're not ready?" You might ask them, "What would it take to make you ready?" They may say they don't know enough.

Review with them the benefits of receiving Christ and share your personal testimony. Offer to meet with them again. If they are interested, they will agree to meet with you. Consider going through the Gospel of John with them.

There Are Too Many Hypocrites in the Church

Agree with them. Say, "There is no perfect church because there are no perfect people." If you were to join a perfect church, it wouldn't be perfect anymore. We're all hypocrites in a way because we all fall short of living up to all of God's commands. The only people who will get to heaven are forgiven people. The only perfect person who ever lived is Jesus. That's why Christ came. He came to die for our sins and offer us forgiveness of all our sins. Would you like to receive the Lord's offer of love and forgiveness for your sins?

I'm a Good Person

Ask, "Have you obeyed all of God's commands?" James 2:10 says, "For whoever keeps the whole law and yet stumbles in one point, he has become guilty of all." Some other scriptures to share are Romans 3:10; 3:23; James 4:17; Matthew 5:48; Isaiah 64:6, and the ten commandments to show we're all guilty before a holy God. But God offers complete forgiveness, and He paid the full price for all our sins. After sharing these verses with them, ask them if they would like to receive the Lord's offer of forgiveness.

I Tried That, but It Didn't Work for Me

Ask them what they have tried. What church did they go to? Maybe it was a liberal church or a cult. Maybe they got baptized or prayed the prayer to receive Christ but never really understood what they were doing (that happened to me). It's possible they don't really know what it means to be born again. Ask them if they would like to make sure they know God personally and review the gospel with them. Some may have been exposed to a Bible-believing church and the gospel, but now they are living in sin—viewing pornography, taking drugs, and so on. They may have had parents who distorted the gospel by their lives, and now they are in rebellion against God. Review the gospel with them and share with them the story of the prodigal son—that God, like a perfect, loving Father, is there for them to return to Him like the story Jesus tells in Luke 15.

15

MAKE DISCIPLES

The Great Commission is found in Matthew 28:18–20. The main phrase of the Great Commission is "**make disciples**." We tell unbelievers the good news and then help those who believe in Christ to grow in their faith.

Some churches prioritize evangelism, while others prioritize discipleship. These are like two wings on an airplane. Lifeway Research says biblical disciple-making involves the whole process of winning the lost, building the believer, equipping the worker, and sending out proven multipliers.

Paul said in 2 Timothy 2:2 (ESV), "The things which you have heard from me in the presence of many witnesses, entrust these to faithful men who will be able to teach others also." There are four generations of discipleship in this verse: (1) Paul's own generation, (2) Timothy's generation, (3) the people Timothy will teach, and (4) the ones they will teach and disciple.

Today, there are vast resources on the Internet for spiritual growth, including ministries committed to discipleship and disciple-making. Here is a list of resources on discipleship:

- *Master Plan of Evangelism*, a classic book on discipleship.

- Cru has the "10 Basic Steps toward Christian Maturity," which is designed to provide the new believer with a sure foundation of their faith. Cru also has "Transferable Concepts" in print and on video that teaches the principles of the Christian life.

- Since 1933, the Navigators (Navigators.org) have helped people worldwide know Jesus through what is called Life-to-Life Discipleship. It includes a Digital-Discipleship Journey that includes emailing a person on a weekly basis and topics to help you grow spiritually. These and other great resources can be found on their website at www.Navigators.org/resources.

- Bible Study Fellowship (bsfinternational.org) offers free, in-depth Bible studies for men and women to uncover the truths of God's Word together.

Churches should focus on building disciples who are followers and learners of Jesus. Pastor Marc Fournier of Crossroads Bible Church in Bellevue, Washington, says, "All that we do at our church is about building disciples who will bring Jesus to our world and who then build other disciples. Our discipleship pathway includes helping folks get 'planted' in Truth or God's Word. Mature disciples seek to make other disciples as well as serve in our church community."

Canyon Hills Community Church in Bothell, Washington, has as their motto "to make more and better disciples of Jesus Christ." They have a School of Discipleship where they offer courses on topics such as How to Study the Bible, Know What You Believe, Theology, the Life of Christ, and more.

Real-Life Ministries is a church led by Pastor Jim Putman that started with a few people and now has several thousand each week based on a focus on discipleship. Putman's book *Real-Life Discipleship* focuses on true, effective discipleship for churches. *DiscipleShift: Five Shifts to Help Your Church Make Disciples Who Make Disciples* written by Putman and Bobby Harrington is another great resource.

Discipleship.org breaks down these three key parts to what it means to be a disciple:

1. "Following" Jesus (head)
2. "Being changed" by Jesus through the Holy Spirit (heart)
3. "Fishers of men" being committed to the mission of Christ (hands)

JesusOnline Discipleship

JesusOnline Ministries (JOM) helps website visitors and JO Discipleship App users become faithful and fruitful disciples of Jesus Christ. This is an online ministry that helps believers develop a more comprehensive understanding of who Jesus is, what He has done, and what His purpose is for their lives so they can follow Him more wholeheartedly. This online discipleship is not meant to replace or compete against discipleship that takes place in a local church.

Their Strategy

After presenting the gospel, JOM invites visitors to download the free JO App, the primary platform for discipleship. It allows users to communicate directly with the JO App online ministers. Over 500,000 people to date have downloaded this free Jo App.

Their Resources

Those who come to Christ can access on the JO App:

- The Adventure of Living with Jesus
- New Life in Christ
- R.E.C.A.P. Bible Study Method
- Time with God section with devotionals and a Bible study series
- Building Blocks for Maturity with key topics of discipleship
- Share Jesus with articles on evangelism and evangelistic tools
- Facts for Faith with apologetic articles to deepen their faith in Christ

Below are two of the thousands of comments on JOM's online discipleship materials. These comments are from the continent of Africa in particular.

"The discipleship booklet has transformed my life and my understanding about what it is to live for Christ and trust His Word. The Adventure of Living with Jesus discipleship booklet is a real treasure for me!" —Pastor Assah, Togo

"My name is Pastor Stanley Fachi in Malawi. The JO App has helped me be grounded in the

Word of God. I preach to thousands of people every Sunday and also teach about 600 pastors in Malawi and Mozambique. I have printed everything on the JO App, and I have started already making some tracts and sharing them with people. Thanks again for all you've done to encourage and equip me." —Pastor Stanley Fachi, Malawi

Discipleship Is God's Strategy

Jesus told His disciples to teach all that He taught to their disciples. In a few short years, they had "turned the world upside down" (Acts 17:6). Discipleship starts with evangelism, and we should never forget that, but we should always pursue making disciples who will in turn make disciples. To reach the world for Christ, we need to share the gospel to as many people as possible and disciple those who come to Christ. This was the model Jesus commanded in the Great Commission.

Ed Stetzer is an author, speaker, pastor, church planter, Christian missiologist, and Billy Graham's Distinguished Chair of Church Mission and Evangelism at Wheaton College. He summed up the relationship of evangelism and discipleship: "Our evangelism has to be focused on making disciples who become disciple-makers, and our discipleship has to be mission-driven, leading those discipled to share Christ."

True discipleship leads to evangelism, and true evangelism leads to discipleship, which is the Lord's way of reaching the world for His glory.

16
NEXT STEPS AND
FINAL THOUGHTS

Now What?

We are to be involved in the Lord's command to fulfill the Great Commission. It's as simple as ABC.

A—ASK

Ask the Lord to show you who in your life needs Jesus. God has put you in certain people's lives to share the good news with them.

Lee Strobel concludes his book *The Unexpected Adventure* with this challenge: "Whose door is

God telling you to knock on? What phone call do you need to make, or what email do you know you ought to send? Which neighbor . . . what relative . . . who is the old friend you need to reestablish contact with? Ask the Holy Spirit to show you the steps to take—big or small—to engage in the unexpected adventure. Then step out and follow His lead today."

Make a list of perhaps five or more friends, family, neighbors, coworkers, or social media connections who need Jesus, and commit them to the Lord in prayer.

B—BASIC STRATEGY

1. Get Trained

Learn how to share your faith at your church or from a parachurch ministry. Select a gospel method that you prefer and develop your personal testimony so you can share it at anytime and anywhere.

"We proclaim to you the one who existed from the beginning, whom we have heard and seen. We saw him with our own eyes and touched him with our own hands. He is the Word of life" (1 John 1:1 NLT).

2. Memorize Key Scriptures

Pick five or more of these 11 verses to memorize so you can share your faith and repeat them on a regular basis.

- **Romans 3:23 (ESV):** "For all have sinned and fall short of the glory of God."

- **Romans 5:8 (ESV):** "But God shows his love for us in that while we were still sinners, Christ died for us."

- **Romans 6:23 (ESV):** "For the wages of sin is death, but the free gift of God is eternal life in Christ Jesus our Lord."

- **John 3:3 (ESV):** Jesus said: "Truly, truly, I say to you, unless one is born again, he cannot see the kingdom of God."

- **John 14:6 (ESV):** "Jesus said to him, 'I am the way, and the truth, and the life. No one comes to the Father except through me.'"

- **Romans 10:9–10 (ESV):** "If you confess with your mouth that Jesus is Lord and believe in your heart that God raised him from the dead, you will be saved."

- **John 3:16 (ESV):** "For God so loved the world, that He gave His only begotten Son, that whoever believes in Him shall not perish, but have eternal life."

- **Revelation 3:20 (ESV):** "Behold I stand at the door and knock. If anyone opens the door, I will come into him and eat with him, and he with Me."

- **John 1:12 (ESV):** "But to all who did receive him, who believed in his name, he gave the right to become children of God."

- **Ephesians 2:8–9 (ESV):** "For by grace you have been saved through faith; and this is not of yourselves, it is the gift of God; not a result of works, so that no one may boast."

- **I John 5:11–12 (ESV):** "And this is the testimony, that God gave us eternal life, and this life is in his Son. Whoever has the Son has life; whoever does not have the Son of God does not have life."

C—COMMIT Your Time and Resources to Fulfilling the Great Commission

Here are Jesus's final words before ascending to the Father: "All authority has been given to Me in heaven and on earth. Go therefore and make disciples of all the nations, baptizing them in the name of the Father and the Son and the Holy Spirit, teaching them to observe all that I commanded you; and lo, I am with you always, even to the end of the age" (Matthew 28:18–20).

Read a book on evangelism that includes discipleship as a strategy to fulfill the Great Commission. There are many ways to strategically reach people for Christ in our day and age. One of the most cost-effective ways is through the Internet. Today it's possible to reach people with the gospel in nearly every country of the world for as little as three cents. A ministry my wife and I personally support—JesusOnline.com—is seeing people indicate decisions for Christ for under 50 cents each.

Phil Wiegand, a business investor and author, wrote, "Whenever I invest my treasure in His Kingdom, I am storing up treasure in heaven that will last for eternity. A few years ago, I became aware of the tremendously effective outreach JesusOnline is having around the world on the Internet. . . . It took me a nano-second to decide I wanted to get in on this eternal investment opportunity."

Whatever ministry you choose, invest your financial resources to proclaim the extravagant news of the gospel that will echo into eternity.

It Only Takes a Spark to Get a Fire Going

Have you ever heard of Mordecai Ham? Mordecai came to Charlotte, North Carolina, to put on an evangelistic crusade. A sandy-haired young man named Billy Frank heard Mordecai preach. Frank responded to the invitation, was converted, and became known as Billy Franklin Graham who probably preached to more people than any other person who has ever lived.

Who knows? The next Billy Graham may be someone you share Christ with and later gives their life to Christ. God has placed you and me at a certain place at a certain time to make an eternal impact for others.

The Story of Charles Peace

Charlie Peace was an English burglar and murderer who embarked on a life of crime. In 1879, he was arrested and taken on the death-walk to be hung. A prison chaplain routinely read some Bible verses, and Charlie Peace was shocked at the way the chaplain showed no emotion when reading about hell. Could this preacher believe the words that there is an eternal fire? This was too much for Charlie Peace. "Sir," he said, addressing the preacher, "if I believed what you and the church of God say that you believe, even if England were covered with broken glass from coast to coast, I would walk over it, if need be, on hands and knees and think it worthwhile living, just to save one soul from an eternal hell like that!"

Our salvation and the gospel are "things into

which angels long to look" (1 Peter 1:12). Angels who have a front-row seat to God's power and miraculous works are awestruck by the fact that the Son of God laid down His life to save us. There is nothing on earth or in God's universe that can compare to the gospel. During Jesus's triumphal entry into Jerusalem, the Pharisees said to Him, "Teacher, rebuke Your disciples." But Jesus answered, "I tell you, if these become silent, the stones will cry out" (Luke 19:39–40). Let's not become silent. Let's proclaim the most amazing news ever to the world.

In Luke 14:15–24 Jesus tells the parable of the great banquet to show how God is graciously extending His invitation to everyone. Many of those invited to the banquet made excuses not to come. The head of the household then invited "the poor and crippled and blind and lame" so that his house would be filled. God is inviting everyone to His eternal home. Someday perhaps very soon, the entry door to God's great invitation into Heaven will be closed.

Revelation 22:17 says: "The Spirit and the bride say, 'Come.' And let the one who hears say, 'Come.' And let the one who is thirsty come; let the one who wishes would take the water of life without cost."

May God grant us the courage to faithfully witness to those who don't know Christ before the door to heaven is eternally closed.

SCRIPTURE INDEX

RESOURCES

Books on Evangelism and Discipleship

- *One Heartbeat Away* by Mark Cahill
- *Evangelism and the Sovereignty of God* by J. I. Packer
- *One Thing You Can't Do in Heaven* by Mark Cahill
- *Good News for a Change* by Matt Mikalatos
- *Bringing the Gospel Home* by Randy Newman
- *Organic Outreach* by Kevin Harney
- *The Unexpected Adventure* by Lee Strobel and Mark Mittelberg
- *Tell Someone* by Greg Laurie
- *How to Talk about Jesus* by Sam Chan
- *How to Give Away Your Faith* by Paul Little.
- *Becoming a Contagious Church* by Mark Mittleberg
- *Becoming a Contagious Christian* by Bill Hybels and Mark Mittelberg

- *Turning Everyday Conversations into Gospel Conversations* by Bennett Leslie and Steve Wright
- *Digital Evangelism* by Jeffrey Akers
- *e-Vangelism* by Martin Luther Quick
- *The Art of Neighboring* by Jay Pathak and Dave Runyon
- *Sharing the Gospel with Ease* by Thom S. Rainer
- *The Evangelist* by Richard D. Phillips
- *Share Jesus without Fear* by William Fay
- *Questioning Evangelism* by Randy Newman
- *Compelled—The Irresistible Call to Share Your Faith* by Dudley Rutherford
- *Not Beyond Reach* by Aaron Pierce
- *Evangelism That Works* by George Barna
- *Street Smarts* by Gregory Koukl
- *Tactics* by Gregory Koukl
- *Master Plan of Evangelism* by Robert Coleman
- *Real-Life Discipleship* by Jim Putman
- *Discipleship Shift: Five Shifts to Help Your Church Make Disciples* by Jim Putman and Bobby Harrington
- *Discipleship Essentials* by Greg Ogden

Books for Sharing with Jewish People

- *A Rabbi Looks at Jesus of Nazareth* by Jonathan Bernis
- *A Rabbi Looks at the Last Days* by Jonathan Bernis
- *Betrayed* by Stan Telchin

Resources for Sharing with Muslims

- *Seeking Allah, Finding Jesus* by Nabeel Qureshi
- *No God but One—Allah or Jesus?* by Nabeel Qureshi
- *Glad News! God Loves You My Muslim Friend* by Samy Tanagho
- *A Christian's Pocket Guide to Islam* by Patrick Sookhdeo
- *Answering Islam* at www.answering-islam.org
- *Dreams and Visions: Is Jesus Awakening the Muslim World?* by Tom Doyle
- *The Islam Debate* by Josh McDowell
- *The Camel—How Muslims Are Coming to Christ* by Kevin Greeson
- *Son of Hamas* by Mosab Hassan Yousef
- *Standing in the Fire* by Tom Doyle Standin

Resources for Sharing with Hindus and Buddhists

Sharing Christ with Hindus by Madasamy Thirumalai

- Marg Network Website
- *Disciple Making Among Hindus* by Tim Shultz
- *Christian Barriers to Jesus* by Paul Pennington
- *Connecting With Hindu International Students* by W Stephens
- *Ten Tips for Ministering to Hindus* by HL Richard
- *Is The Commission Still Great* by Steve Richardson

Sharing Your Faith with a Buddhist by Madasamy Thirumalai

Resources on Apologetics

- *A New Kind of Evangelism* by Sean McDowell
- *Evidence That Demands a Verdict* by Josh McDowell
- *The Case for Christ* by Lee Strobel
- *The Case for Faith* by Lee Strobel
- *The Case for the Creator* by Lee Strobel

- *Mere Christianity* by C. S. Lewis
- *Cold-Case Christianity* by J. Warner Wallace
- *I Don't Have Enough Faith to Be an Atheist* by Norman Geisler
- *Apologetics Study Bible* by Broadman & Holman Publishers
- *The Reason for God: Belief in an Age of Skepticism* by Timothy Keller
- *Answers to Tough Questions Skeptics Ask about the Christian Faith* by Josh McDowell and Don Stewart
- *When Skeptics Ask* by Norman Geisler and Ronald Brooks
- *The Kingdom of the Cults* by Walter Martin
- *Fast Facts on False Teaching* by Ron Carlson and Ed Decker
- *A Different Gospel* by Dan McConnell and Hank Hanegraff
- *Reason to Believe* by R. C. Sproul
- *Letters from a Skeptic* by Dr. Gregory A. Boyd and Edward K. Boyd
- *The Story of Reality* by Gregory Koukl

- *God Doesn't Believe in Atheists* by Ray Comfort

- *Is God Real?* by Lee Strobel

Web Resources

- www.josh.org/resources/apologetics/answering-skeptics/

- www.gotquestions.org/questions_apologetics.html

- www.Y-Jesus.com

- Apologetics315.com

- Summit Ministries (www.summit.org)

- "Does God Exist?" William Lane Craig vs. Christopher Hitchens Debate

WEBSITES, DVDs, UTUBE, AND APPS

- JO App by JesusOnline Ministries—downloaded by millions with vast resources on evangelism, apologetics, discipleship, and more. View the app at app.JesusOnline.com, or download it at Jesus Online.com/app.

- GodTools by Cru—training on how to share your faith, the Four Spiritual Laws, Knowing God Personally, and other tools for Christian growth

- Y-Jesus.com, Jesusonline.com, and Jesusonlineministries.com

- *Francis Chan's video "Just Stop and Think"—an excellent 15-minute presentation of the gospel.* https://www.youtube.com/watch?v=pRi4VwcrYmA

- Gospel Coalition website: thegospelcoalition.org

- Outreachmagazine.com—ideas, resources, and innovations for Christian leaders and churches

Witnessing Tools and Resources

- "Eternal Answers to Life's Most Important Questions"—tract

- "The Gift of Heaven—5 Keys to God's Incredible Offer"—tract

- "One Second after You . . . " by Mark Cahill—an excellent 62-page booklet; order at: www.markcahill.org

- "Two Ways to Live"—tract (http://www.matthiasmedia.com.au/2wtl)

SURVEYS

Evangelistic surveys can be effective in sharing the gospel. Here are a few samples from a church in Washington state that uses them when they visit malls, parks, and bus stations to engage people in conversations about the gospel.

Christmas Survey

1. What would you say is the meaning of Christmas?
   - It's a family holiday.
   - It's a time to party/enjoy your friends.
   - It's a time to celebrate the birth of Jesus Christ.
   - It's a religious holiday.
   - Other: _____

2. What is the most meaningful part of the holidays to you?
   - Time spent with my family.
   - Time to enjoy the fun and festivities of the season.
   - Time to enjoy friends and activities.
   - I like to go to church and celebrate the meaning of Christmas.
   - Other: _____

3. In what ways does celebrating Christmas impact you?
   - It makes me a more giving person.
   - I volunteer to help others in need.
   - I am happier and more optimistic.

- It fills me with joy and gives meaning to life.
- I love giving gifts to others.
- Other: _____

4. Christmas commemorates the birth of Jesus Christ. To you, who is Jesus Christ?
   - Prophet
   - Myth
   - Son of God
   - Savior of the world
   - Other: _____

Easter Survey

1. To you, what is the meaning of Easter?

_____

_____

_____

_____

2. In what ways do you celebrate Easter?
   - Gather with family for a meal.
   - Get together with friends.
   - Take the day off to relax.
   - Do a fun activity.
   - Go to church.
   - Other: _____

3. Why in your opinion is Easter an important holiday?
   - It's something that is always done.
   - It brings families closer together.
   - It gives us something spiritual to think about.
   - It is the resurrection of Jesus Christ.
   - Other: _____

4. Do you have any spiritual belief in your life?

_____

_____

_____

_____

_____

_____

_____

_____

5. To you, who is Jesus?

_____

_____

_____

_____

_____

_____

_____

_____

General Spiritual Interest Questionnaire

1. What is your spiritual/church background?

_____

_____

_____

_____

_____

2. How much of the Bible have you read?

   ❏ All
   ❏ More than half
   ❏ Less than half
   ❏ None

3. To you, who is Jesus?

_____

_____

_____

_____

_____

4. Let's suppose you were to die tonight and stand before God. If He asked you, "Why should I let you into heaven?" what would you tell Him?

   ❑ I tried to be a good person and follow the rules.

   ❑ I haven't sinned.

   ❑ Jesus is my Savior.

   ❑ Other: _____

5. On a scale of 1 to 100, how would you rate your certainty of going to heaven?

   ❑ 0–49%

   ❑ 50–74%

   ❑ 75–99%

   ❑ 100%

   ❑ No clue

6. May I get your opinion on a brief outline that explains how you can be certain of going to heaven and how to know God in a personal way?

   _____

   _____

   _____

   _____

Future Events Survey

Date: _____   Name: _____

1. What concerns you most about the major challenges facing our world in the future?

   ❑ World War

   ❑ Famine

   ❑ Israel/Middle East

   ❑ Other _____

2. If you were to die by a disease like COVID or from nuclear war, where would you go?

   ❑ Heaven

   ❑ Hell

   ❑ Don't know

   ❑ Other

3. On a scale of 1 to 100, how certain would you be to get to heaven? _____%.

4. Do you know what the Bible says in order to get to heaven?

   ❑ No

   ❑ Yes

5. May I share with you the general entrance requirements for heaven based on what the Bible says?

❏ Yes

❏ No

❏ Already know

Romans 3:23; Romans 6:23; Ephesians 2:8–9; John 14:6; John 3:16; 2 Corinthians 5:21; Romans 10:9–10; Revelation 3:20; 1 John 5:11–12

COMMENTS:

_____

_____

_____

_____

_____

_____

_____

_____

_____

Dave and Bonnie Chapman currently live in Kirkland, Washington.

If you would like to connect with Dave, you may email him at ExtraordinaryEvangelism@gmail.com

www.ingramcontent.com/pod-product-compliance
Lightning Source LLC
Chambersburg PA
CBHW070026100426
42740CB00013B/2610